More ORIGAMI

The Art of Paper-Folding

ROBERT HARBIN

Hodder Paperbacks

To
The Memory
of
Ligia Montoya
of
Argentina

First Printed 1971
Hodder Paperback Edition
Copyright © 1971
Robert Harbin
Second Impression 1971
Third Impression 1971

ISBN 0 340 15384 9
Printed in Great Britain for Hodder Paperbacks Ltd.,
by Richard Clay (The Chaucer Press), Ltd.
Bungay, Suffolk

PREFACE

Origami in paperback has, thanks to you, dear enthusiasts, been an unqualified success and is in fact a bestseller.

The appeal of Origami as an intellectual pastime for young and old is now so great that I have done my best to provide, for experts and beginners alike, a further collection of exciting folds in the shape of *More Origami*.

Because I am an Origami addict myself I have tried to give you as wide a selection as possible, generously provided by folders from all parts of the world. May I add that the selection would have been even wider had it not been for a Post Office strike which happened at the time of writing.

If you are paper-folding for the first time you will be well advised to get hold of a copy of *Origami* (Hodder Paperbacks), because although this book is complete within itself the two books are even more so.

As Origami gains popularity as an art form, certain names are becoming important among the faithful. America is producing some outstanding material and a long list of creative folders, so I hope I will be forgiven if I only mention the two giants of Origami, Neal Elias and Frederick Rohm, who have made such a staggering contribution.

In the months to come I hope to be allowed to produce two mighty tomes featuring creations of the two masters named above.

Fine folds are coming from Great Britain—watch for Eric Kenneway. From the Argentine we have the wonderful collection of folds by the late and much beloved Ligia Montoya; from Spain and the Latin countries emerges the name of Adolfo Cerceda; from Hong Kong, Philip Shen; from Switzerland, Dr. Emanuel Mooser; and from the birthplace of Origami, Japan, a very long list dominated by Akira Yoshizawa.

I must take this opportunity of thanking television viewers for their interest in my Origami programme, and it may be gratifying to know that the same series is being screened in Sweden.

So . . . spread the news about this delightful diversion, so inexpensive, so relaxing, and so challenging.

London   ROBERT HARBIN

CONTENTS

INTRODUCTION

Origami stands poised midway between art and game. It is an art bound by strict and simple rules like those of a game; or it is a game that can produce a work of art. Origami resembles a chess problem on the one hand, and the act of musical composition on the other. Because it has rules, and because the field of action is limited from the start, Origami is an activity in which perfection is attainable.

The creation of a successful Origami figure requires, of course, an extraordinary ingenuity; any good model is a little marvel of engineering, a triumph of imagination over limitations. In the words of the sculptor and painter George Rhoads: 'The beauty of Origami is the beauty of economy. Everything is put to good use—no idle points are hidden away, there is no clumsy thickness, no complex device that could be simplified.' This beauty of economy—the perfect matching of means to ends—is the beauty of fine engineering, and it is hardly too much to say that Origami is a technological art form.

The ingenuity embodied in Origami explains, perhaps, the strength of its appeal to those who love cleverness for its own sake: not only engineers, but magicians, puzzle-solvers, computer programmers, mathematicians, readers of science fiction—all of whom delight in the elegant solution or the revelation of an unexpected consequence of an idea. And it is perhaps the combination of strict rules with hard thinking that accounts for the presence of theologians such as Robert Neale and Philip Shen and philosophers such as Miguel de Unamuno and Koshio Uchiyama among the creators of Origami models. The appeal of Origami, however, is universal. The elemental square becomes as if by magic a highly developed logical structure—an ornament, a toy, a piece of sculpture. Something is conjured up from nothing. Children, who know a good thing when they see it, are invariably fascinated by Origami, and the folding of a piece of paper has many times served as an ice-breaker among the most sophisticated adults.

It is easy to understand the steadily growing popularity of Origami. Folding is a challenging and enjoyable process in itself, and the finished product is attractive. No tools are needed, the materials cost little, and there is nothing to clean up.

Any beginner naturally supposes that there is a vast tradition in China and Japan, and that the East must be filled with creators of Origami figures. This is not the case. The tradition, though it stretches back for centuries, consists of a static repertory of a few dozen excellent figures (and others less distinguished); and though folding has its place in etiquette, it is considered to be an occupation suitable primarily for children. As Philip Shen remarks: 'Origami, like any other art, must be constantly renewed by creative experimentation—and the recent Western achievements may, in a sense, give paper-folding back to China.'

Yoshizawa and Uchiyama, working essentially in isolation, have, to be sure, done much to revitalise the Japanese tradition. But today the great majority of new figures—there are hundreds of them, with more being devised all the time—are the work of Western folders. It is an interesting situation: an Eastern discipline, somewhat neglected, has been transplanted to the West, where it has taken root and begun to flourish. During recent years, Western folders have set for themselves and then solved a long series of problems, each more difficult than the last. By undertaking to fold complex and seemingly impossible subjects, they have carried Origami to a new level of technical maturity; three-dimensional figures, for example, have become possible through the integration of pleating and box-folding with the technical devices of the Japanese tradition. Standards of style and form have risen steadily, and Origami is beginning to be recognised as a legitimate medium for sculpture: major exhibitions have been held in Seattle and London during the past few months. The line-and-arrow code and the vocabulary used in printed instructions are now well established, and Origami has appeared on television with some regularity in England, France, Sweden, Mexico, and the United States. The British Origami Society, founded by Sidney French, has provided the hobby with a firm organisational framework; the Society, which maintains an Origami library and publishes a journal, has an active and enthusiastic membership. In America there are two periodicals devoted to Origami: *The Origamian* is a quarterly containing news and essays along with instructions for models; *The Flapping Bird* is a monthly devoted exclusively to instructions.

Among the principal influences on the remarkable development of Origami in the West have been the books of Robert Harbin. *Paper Magic*, published in 1956, was the first book in English to attempt a general survey of Origami, the first written from an adult viewpoint for an adult audience, the first to present new creations. (It was also the first important book on Origami to come to my attention; I studied it very thoroughly indeed, and even today I keep a copy always at hand.) *Secrets of Origami*, which appeared in 1963, is a big book in every way, an anthology of old and new models so well planned and so comprehensive that it is universally regarded as a classic. The pocket-sized *Origami*, which followed in 1969, reflects in miniature the pattern of its predecessors—something new with something old—and it has reached a large public, thanks to the missionary work of Mr. Harbin's television broadcasts. It is a pleasure to introduce *More Origami*. May it have many sequels!

Wauwatosa, Wisconsin   SAMUEL RANDLETT
March 1971

The Flapping Bird

An Origami Monthly.
Published by
Jay Marshall,
5082 N. Lincoln Ave.,
Chicago, Illinois 60625.

The Origamian

An Origami Quarterly.
Published by
Lillian Oppenheimer,
The Origami Centre,
71 West Eleventh Street,
New York 2, N.Y., U.S.A.

Suppliers of Origami paper:—

John Maxfield,
9 The Broadway,
Mill Hill,
London, N.W.7.

The Secretary, British Origami Society, 33 Fleming Road, Quinton, Birmingham 32.

THE ESSENTIALS
OF ORIGAMI

You will be anxious to go ahead and start work on the models in this book. First, though, there is some helpful information to be considered, and the following essential instructions must be read carefully.

It is a fact that most beginners are not able to follow diagrams and instructions easily and successfully, however carefully they may have been planned. As a rule, Origami illustrators try to cram into each page as much information as possible. This practice is welcomed by the enthusiast and the expert, because it means that the book will be able to explain a large number of models. Unfortunately, though, a page filled with diagrams completely bewilders most beginners.

I have borne this in mind while preparing this book, and you will notice that the earlier pages have been designed with no more than two or three diagrams per page. All the diagrams are clearly drawn, and contain helpful instructions and symbols to give you all possible help, and to explain the mainly standard models which bring you in touch with most of the Basic Folds.

A Basic Fold is a fold from which many models can be made. There are many Basic Folds, both ancient and modern, and this book introduces you to some entirely new ones.

Always fold carefully, accurately, and neatly. If you fold carelessly, the result will be disastrous.

Study each diagram showing the complete folded model. Then, and only then, place your Origami paper in front of you and make your first fold.

When you make a fold, always crease the paper firmly with the back of your thumbnail. Good creases make folding easy, and are an invaluable guide later in the model, when you are making a series of folds.

Pre-creasing is an important feature. Consider, for example, Jack Skillman's Jackstone.

4

Notice how he pre-creases the paper he uses so that everything folds into place at the right moment.

Before you make a Reverse Fold, pre-crease the paper by folding the whole thickness before opening the paper and making the fold (see Reverse Folds).

Notice how paper coloured on one side is used to get the maximum effect for each model. The subject of paper is an important one. Origami paper (which is available from a variety of sources) should be strong, thin, and suitably coloured. But if you cannot lay hands on special Origami paper, almost any paper may be used.

If you are instructed to use a square of paper, make sure that it really is square, and that a rectangle is a true rectangle. Most of the models in this book are based on squares of paper, but there is no regular rule about this, as all shapes of paper can be used, according to the model's needs. See, for example, Ligia Montoya's Xmas Tree.

Origami is not meant to be a simple art. To the expert, it is a challenge to the eye, the brain, and the fingers, a wonderful mental and physical therapy.

When you fold one of the decorations explained in this book, you will find that by altering this or that fold you can invent endless shapes. In fact, you can doodle for hours.

When you have mastered the Basic Folds, you will then be equipped to produce figures and shapes of your own. Have something in mind, and then consider the best Base from which to start. See what you can do with the Neal Elias Figure Base, and Fred Rohm's Simplex Base.

Watch out for terms like Squash Fold. It is so named because you do just that—squash the part indicated so that the sides bulge and it flattens, in most cases symmetrically.

Study the Petal Folds, the Rabbit's Ears, and the various Bases, and try to remember what they are. If you get stuck, have a look at the Contents and refer to the page or pages concerned.

You will notice that certain procedures are used over and over again. You will soon get used to these and be able to carry them out automatically.

When you have folded everything in the first half of the book, you will find that more and more diagrams begin to appear on each page, and that the symbols begin to play a bigger part than the instructions. Many folds are included which have only symbols to guide you and so teach you to use them freely.

Start at the beginning of the book and work your way slowly and steadily through. Do not attempt anything too difficult to start with, because this can only end in disappointment.

If you are making a long train journey, take this book with you and fold a piece of paper to pass the time during your journey. Find a friend with the same interest, and you will both pass many a happy hour.

For the rehabilitation of damaged hands there is nothing like Origami for making reluctant fingers come back to life.

Finally—take it slowly; fold carefully, neatly, and accurately. And START AT THE BEGINNING.

A Note on
SYMBOLS

The symbols used in this book are based on Akira Yoshizawa's code of lines and arrows. Symbols must become second nature to you when folding, but you will find that they are easy to acquire.

The moment you see a line of dashes, you know that the paper must be Valley Folded along that line. When you see a line of dashes and dots, you recognise the sign for a Mountain Fold. To make a Mountain Fold, you naturally turn the paper upside down and make a Valley Fold.

Arrows show the directions in which you must fold: left, right, up, down, in front, behind, and into.

You will notice one arrow which shows that a drawing has been enlarged for clarity. Another arrow indicates that a model must be opened out (see the Jackstone and others). My own special little black arrow indicates that you must sink, press, squeeze, or push in at certain points.

The symbols are in fact self-explanatory. They are simple common sense, and can be learnt in about ten minutes.

Try to use the symbols only and ignore explanations. This will help you when you come to read Japanese Origami books.

Study these symbols carefully

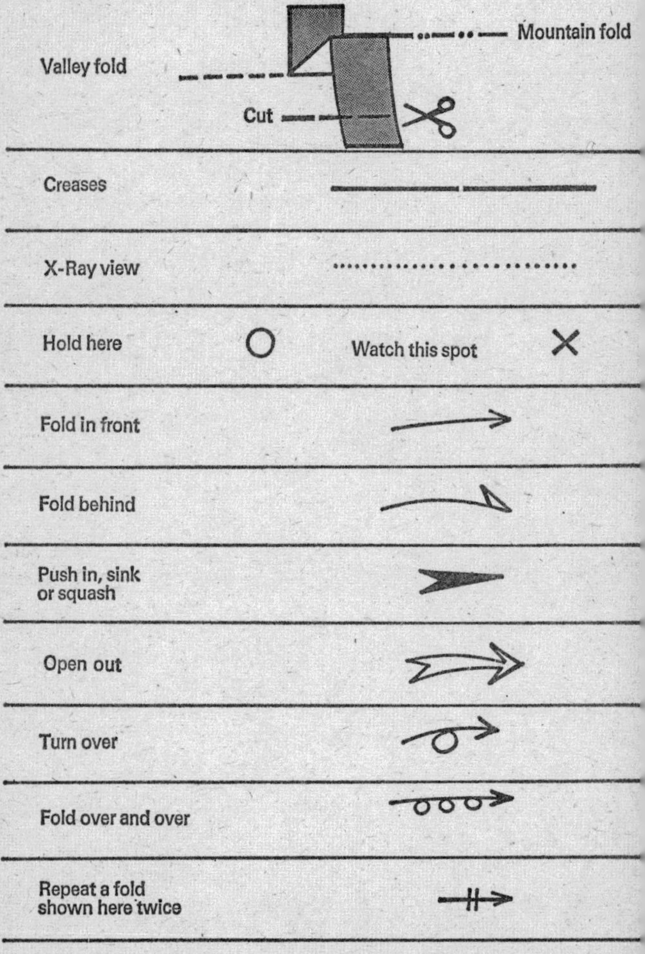

Valley fold

Mountain fold

Cut

Creases

X-Ray view

Hold here ○

Watch this spot ✕

Fold in front

Fold behind

Push in, sink
or squash

Open out

Turn over

Fold over and over

Repeat a fold
shown here twice

8

**These symbols produce a
waterbomb base**

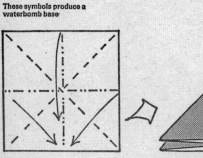

When creased

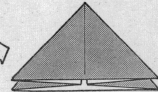

this fold results

**When turned inside out
these folds produce each other**

When creased

this fold results

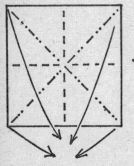

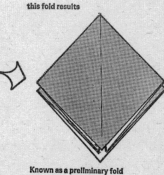

Known as a preliminary fold

Procedures Squash Folds

Marked with symbols like

this →   this   and this

Procedures   Petal Folds

Marked with symbols like

this   this   and this

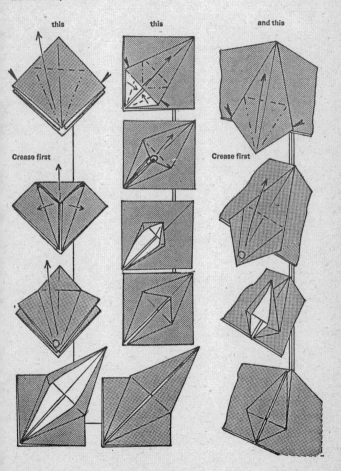

Crease first   Crease first

II

Procedures   Reverse Fold

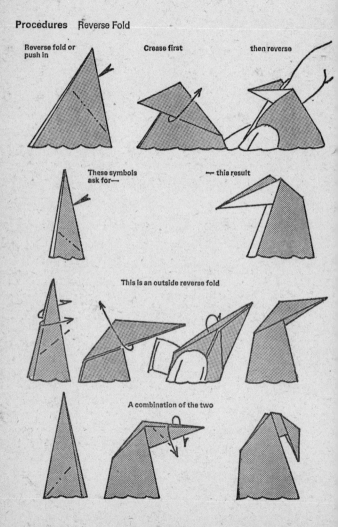

Reverse fold or push in   **Crease first**   **then reverse**

These symbols ask for—   **—this result**

This is an outside reverse fold

A combination of the two

Procedures   Rabbit's Ears

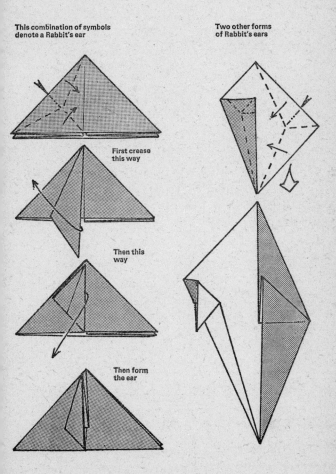

This combination of symbols denote a Rabbit's ear

Two other forms of Rabbit's ears

First crease this way

Then this way

Then form the ear

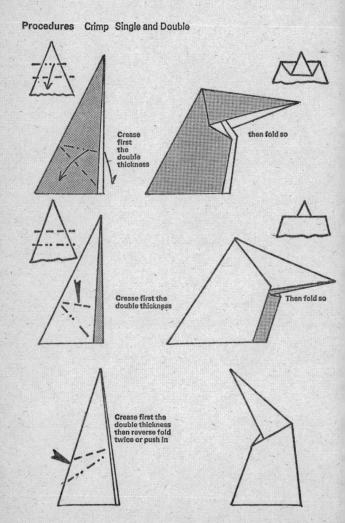

Crease
first
the
double
thickness

then fold so

Crease first the
double thickness

Then fold so

Crease first the
double thickness
then reverse fold
twice or push in

This combination of symbols
means sink

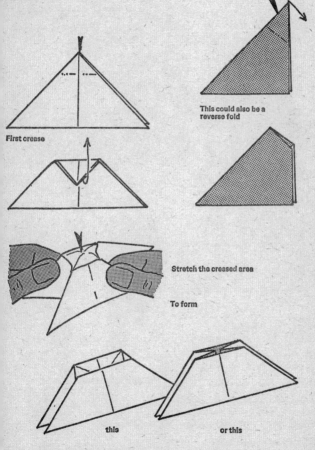

First crease

This could also be a
reverse fold

Stretch the creased area

To form

this   or this

Picture Frame   Florence Temko   America

Use a colourful
paper square

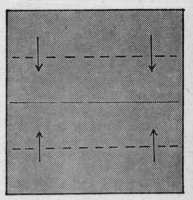

Valley fold flaps

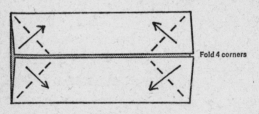

Fold 4 corners

Turn over

Like this

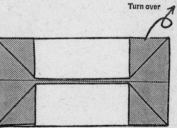

Picture Frame   Put a picture in

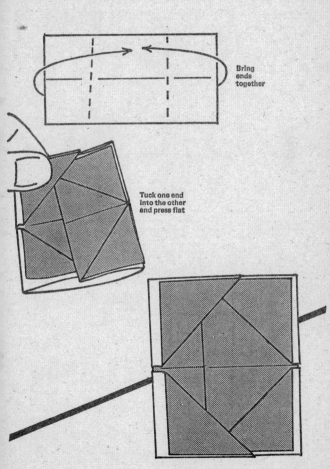

Bring
ends
together

Tuck one end
into the other
and press flat

Dippy Dog   John Smith   England

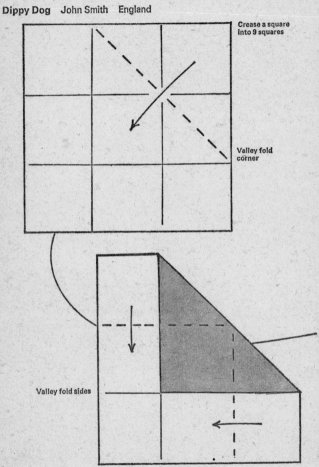

Crease a square
into 9 squares

Valley fold
corner

Valley fold sides

18

Dippy Dog   The Body

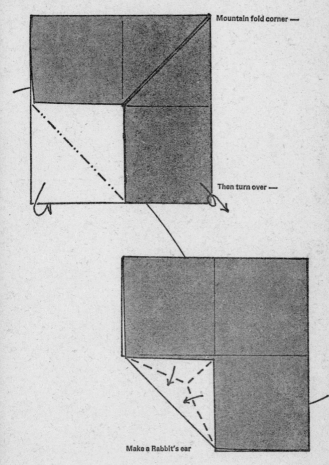

Mountain fold corner —

Then turn over —

Make a Rabbit's ear

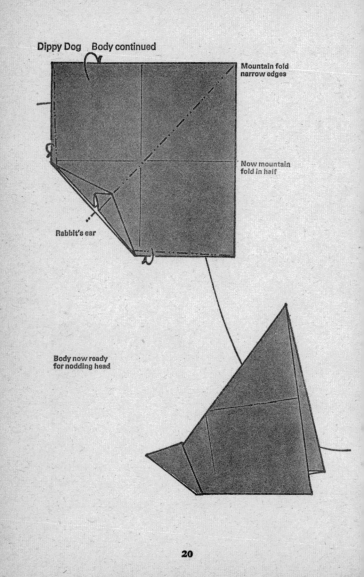

Dippy Dog   Body continued

Mountain fold
narrow edges

Now mountain
fold in half

Rabbit's ear

Body now ready
for nodding head

Dippy Dog   The Head

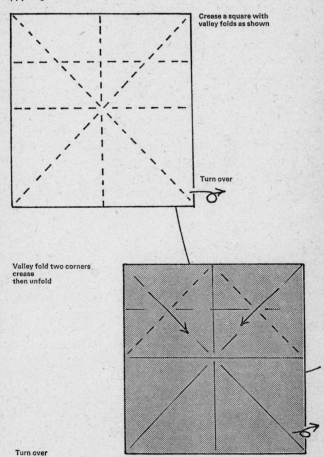

Crease a square with
valley folds as shown

Turn over

Valley fold two corners
crease
then unfold

Turn over

21

Dippy Dog   Head continued

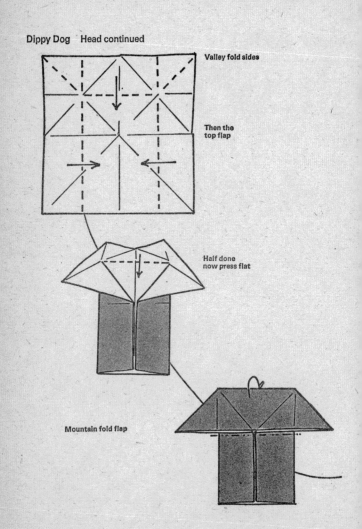

Valley fold sides

Then the
top flap

Half done
now press flat

Mountain fold flap

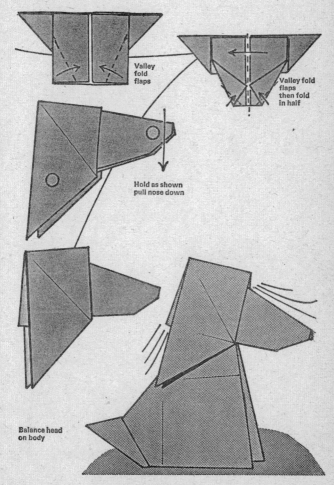

Valley
fold
flaps

Valley fold
flaps
then fold
in half

Hold as shown
pull nose down

Balance head
on body

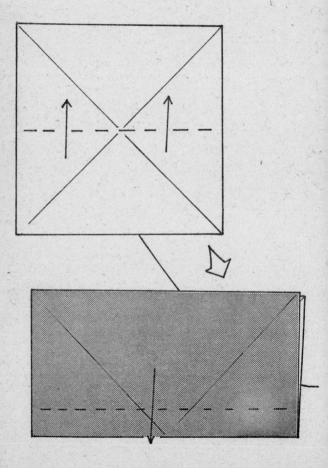

Vase   Symbols only

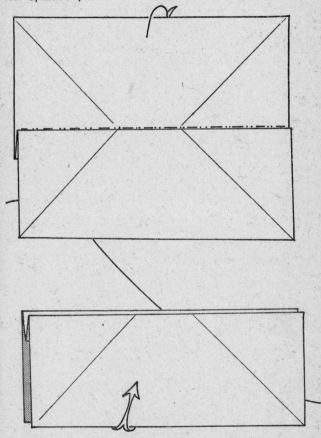

Vase   Note the Repeat signs

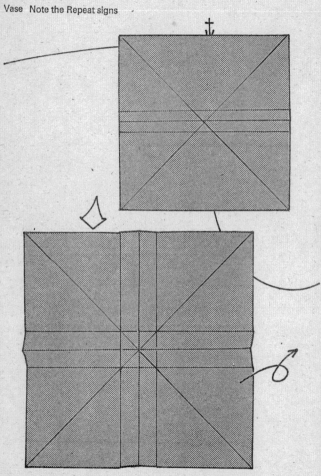

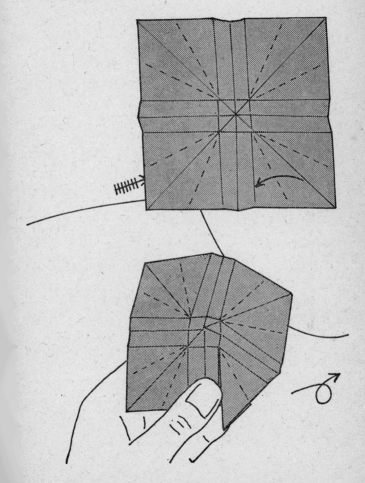

27

Vase   You struggle here

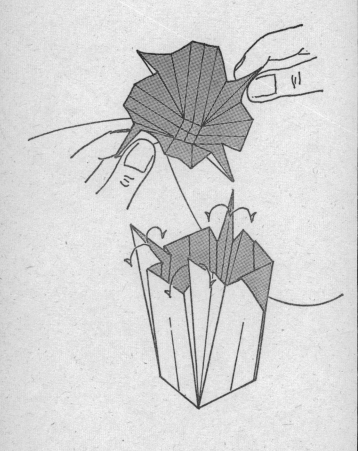

28

Vase Well?

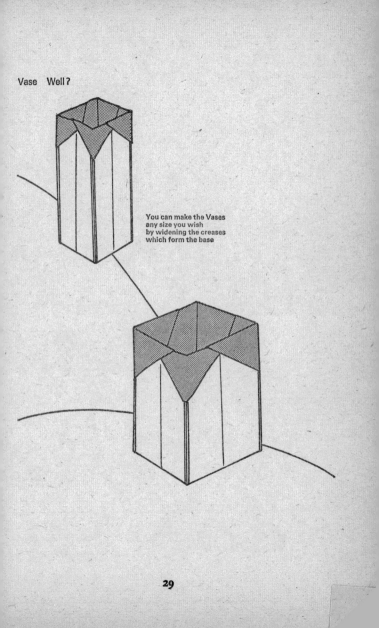

You can make the Vases
any size you wish
by widening the creases
which form the base

Party Hat   David Neale (age 10)   U.S.A.

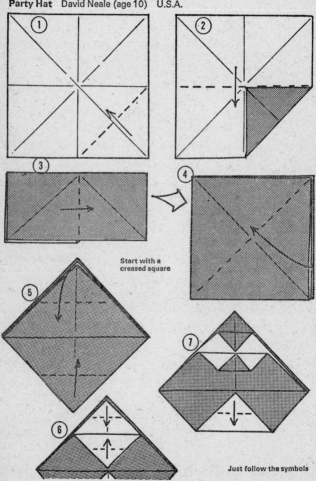

Start with a
creased square

Just follow the symbols

30

Party Hat continued

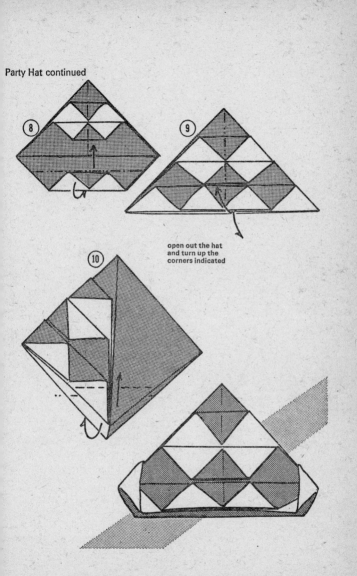

open out the hat
and turn up the
corners indicated

31

Tree   Robert Harbin   England

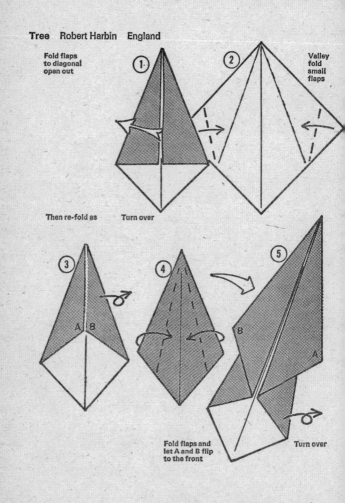

Fold flaps
to diagonal
open out

① ②

Valley
fold
small
flaps

Then re-fold as   Turn over

③ ④ ⑤

A B

B

A

Fold flaps and
let A and B flip
to the front

Turn over

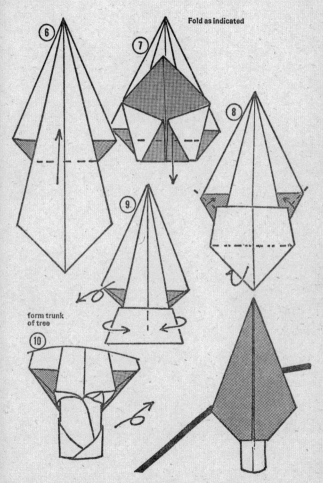

Fold as indicated

form trunk
of tree

Helmet Ligia Montoya Argentina

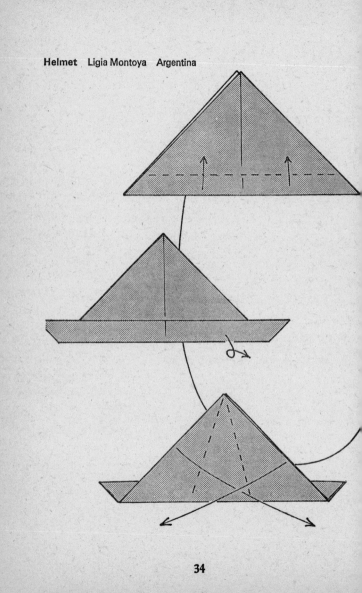

Helmet   One of a large collection

Ocean Liner Peter Johnson (age 10) England

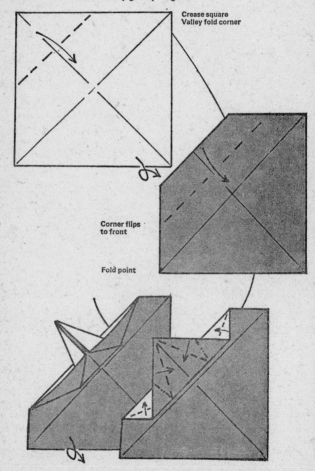

Crease square
Valley fold corner

Corner flips
to front

Fold point

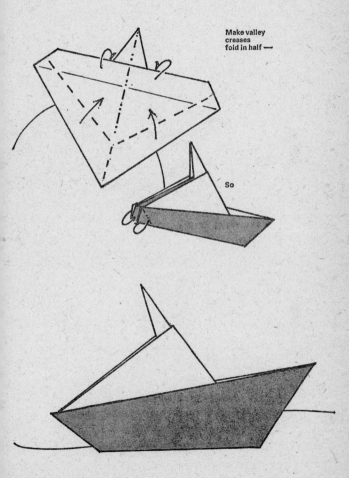

Make valley
creases
fold in half —

So

Noshi   Traditional Japanese

A simple Noshi
which is a good luck
item given with
anything

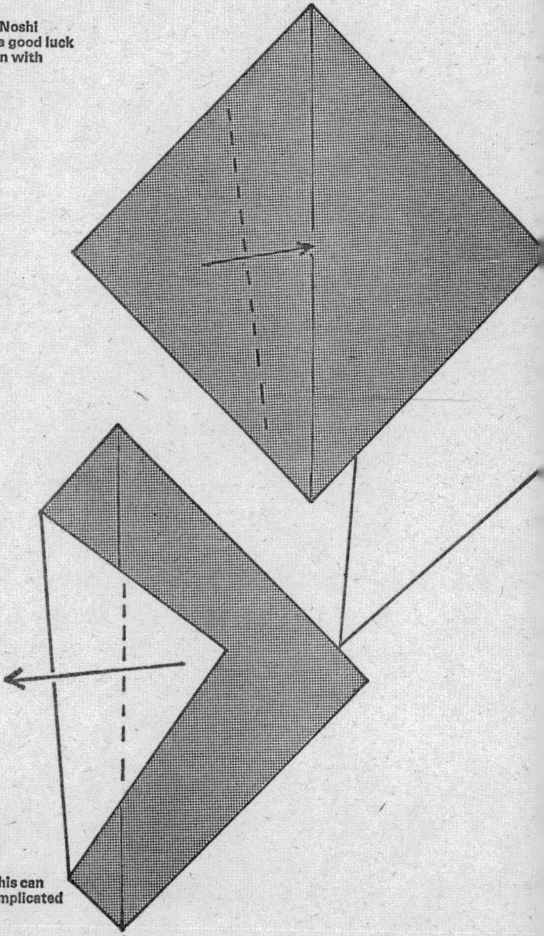

Other Noshis can
be very complicated

Tuck a Noshi
under the ribbon
of a gift

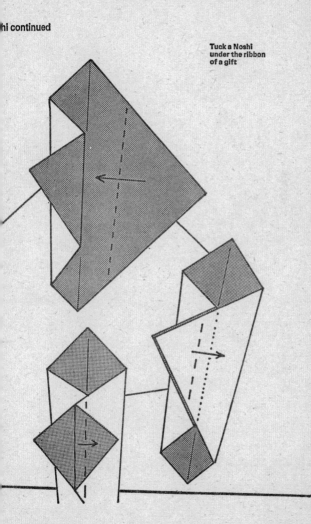

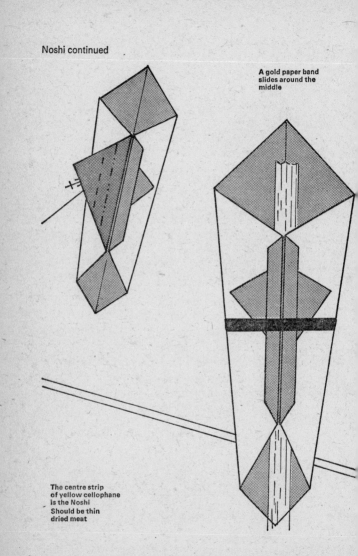

A gold paper band
slides around the
middle

The centre strip
of yellow cellophane
is the Noshi
Should be thin
dried meat

40

Box Double strength

Use a square
grease-proof
if you wish to
use it

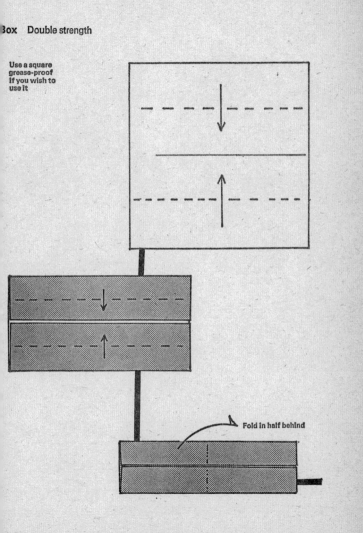

Fold in half behind

Box continued

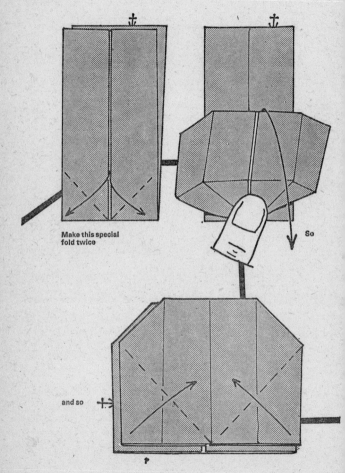

Make this special
fold twice

So

and so

42.

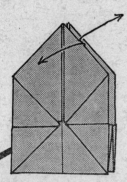

Hold the points
and pull the
box open

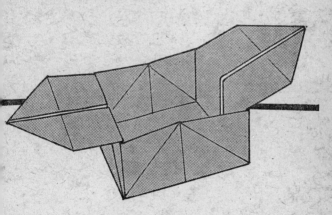

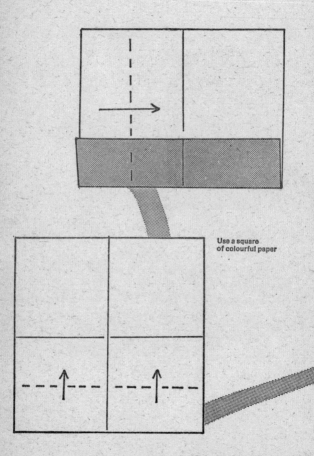

Use a square
of colourful paper

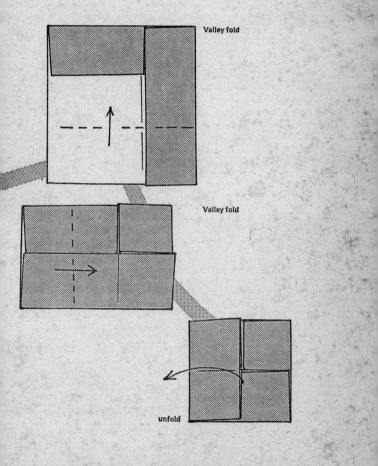

Valley fold

Valley fold

unfold

45

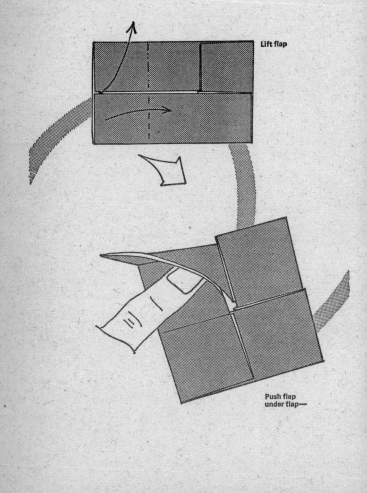

Lift flap

Push flap
under flap—

Decoration continued

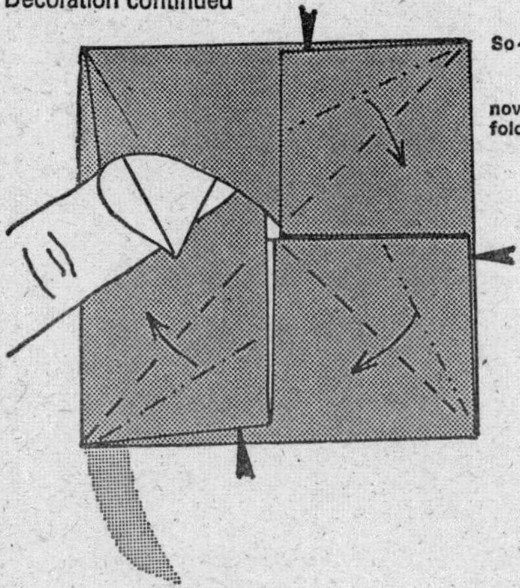

So—

now squash
fold all four corners

(1)

Several squares
fit together
to make patterns

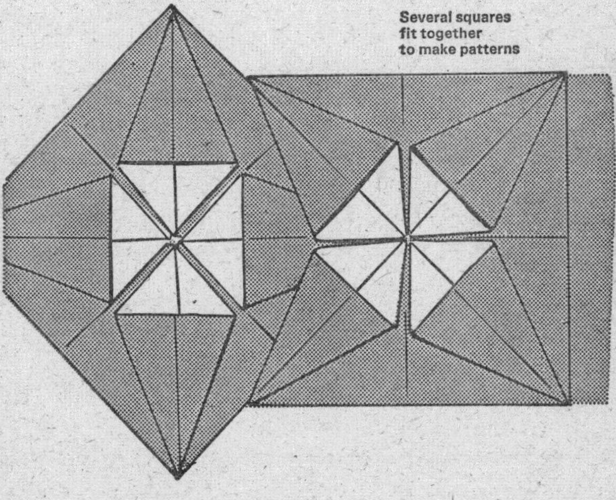

47

Ball   Jack Skillman   U.S.A.

Begin with a square
corners folded
to the middle

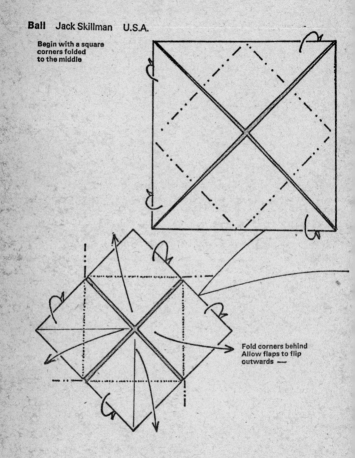

Fold corners behind
Allow flaps to flip
outwards ──

48

= So

Make two of
different colours

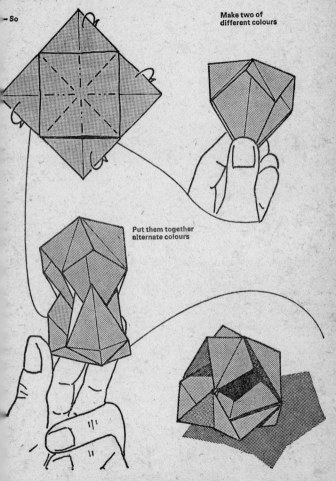

Put them together
alternate colours

Pinwheel   Philip Shen   Hong Kong

Valley fold diagonal creases
crease only
marked lines

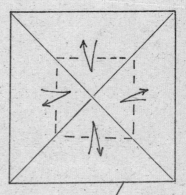

So

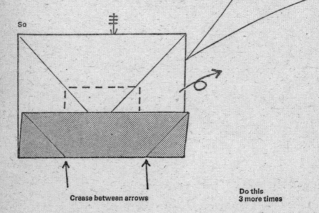

Crease between arrows

Do this
3 more times

50

Pinwheel continued

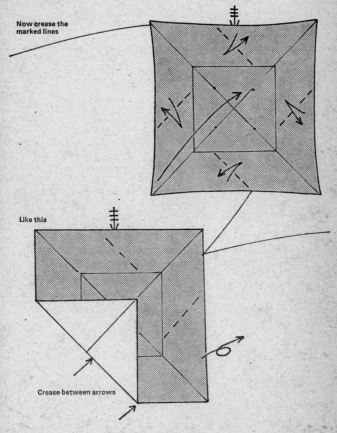

Now crease the
marked lines

Like this

Crease between arrows

Do this 3 more times

Pinwheel continued

Now form the creased square into a pinwheel

So —

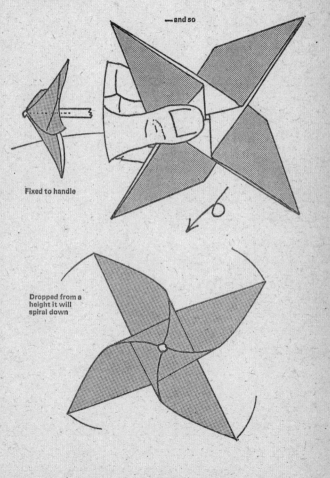

—and so

Fixed to handle

Dropped from a
height it will
spiral down

Double Purse   Endia Saar   America

Crease heavily into thirds
Use striped wrapping paper

Use a
6 x 4
rectangle

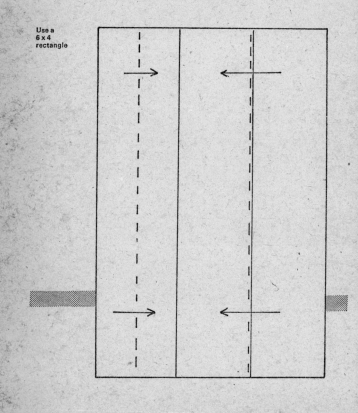

**Valley fold
heavily
into sixths**

**Valley fold
heavily the
seven diagonals**

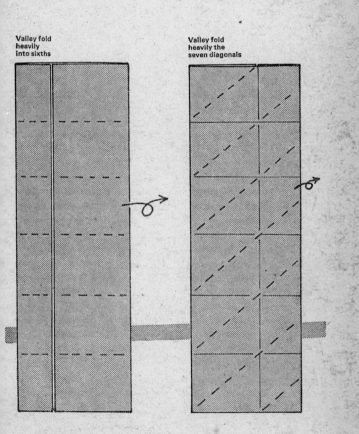

Double Purse continued

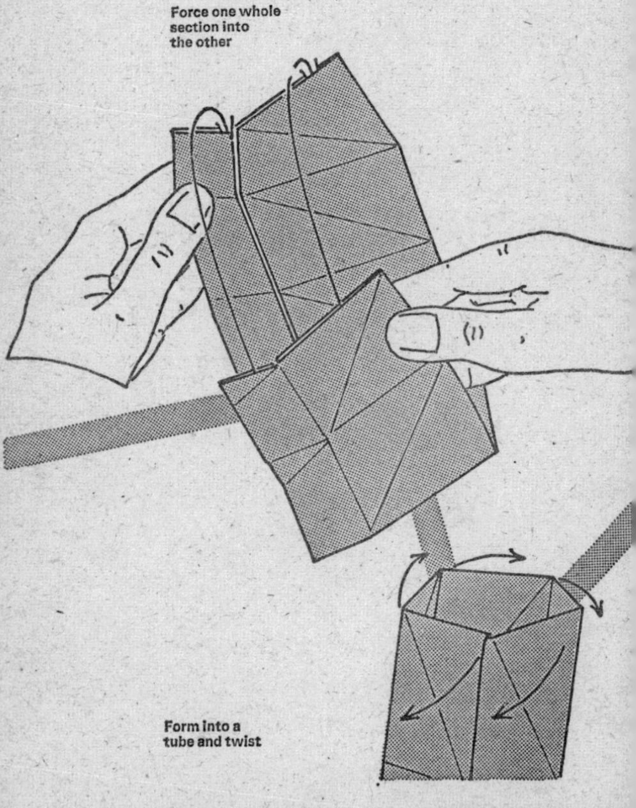
Force one whole section into the other
Form into a tube and twist

The top section
almost flat
Now flatten
the base

Catch the Fly   Alice Gray   U.S.A.

Use a square

Crease one diagonal

Fold the other

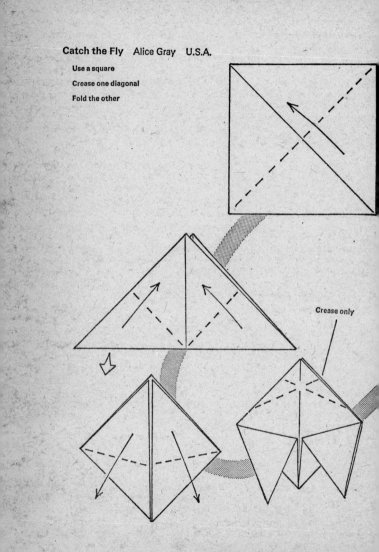

Crease only

58

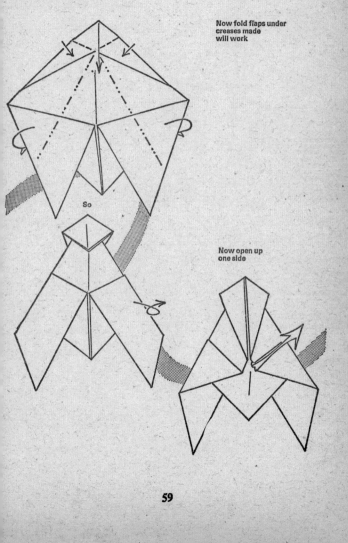

Now fold flaps under
creases made
will work

So

Now open up
one side

59

Catch the Fly continued

—and Valley fold the triangle as you fold side back into place

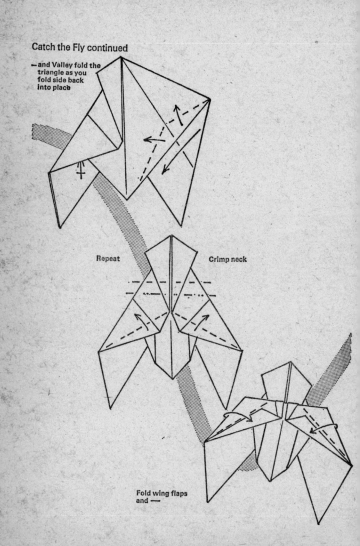

Repeat

Crimp neck

Fold wing flaps and →

Catch the Fly   Did you?

— see how neck folds
come into place

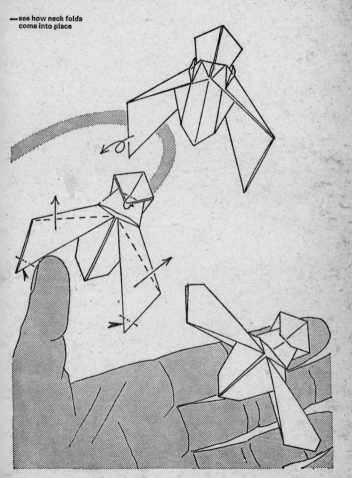

Witch Robert Harbin England

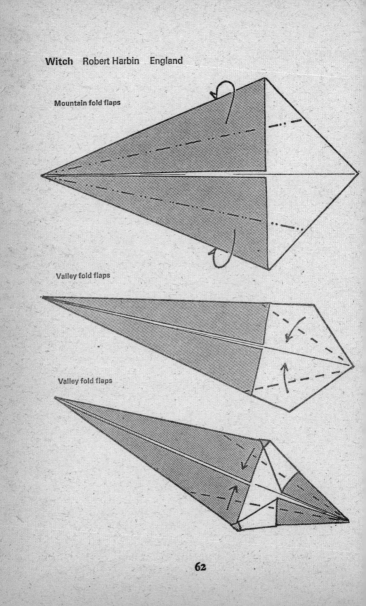

Mountain fold flaps

Valley fold flaps

Valley fold flaps

62

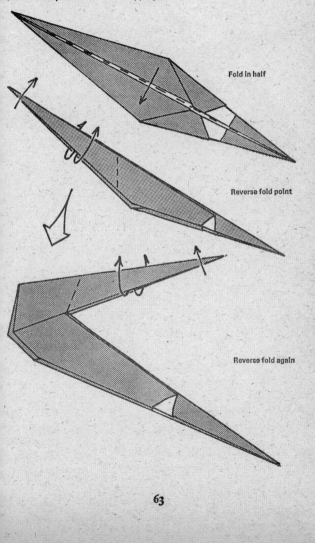

Fold in half

Reverse fold point

Reverse fold again

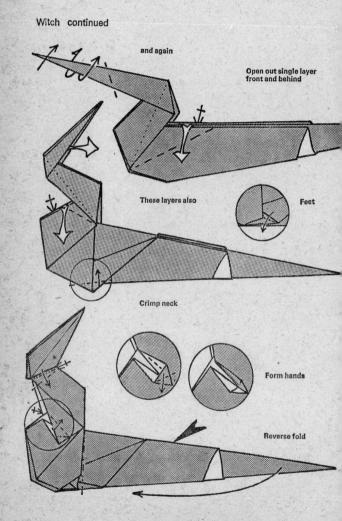

and again

Open out single layer
front and behind

These layers also

Feet

Crimp neck

Form hands

Reverse fold

64

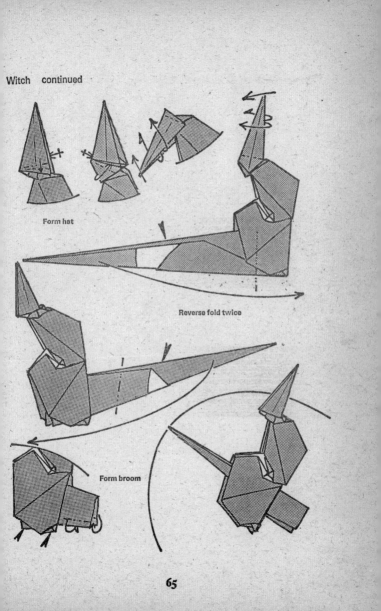

Form hat

Reverse fold twice

Form broom

65

Tropical Bird Ligia Montoya Argentina

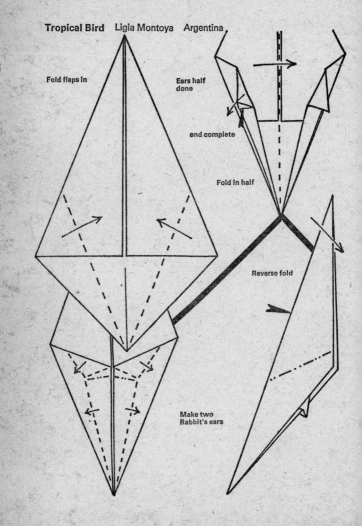

Fold flaps in

Ears half done

and complete

Fold in half

Reverse fold

Make two Rabbit's ears

Tropical Bird continued

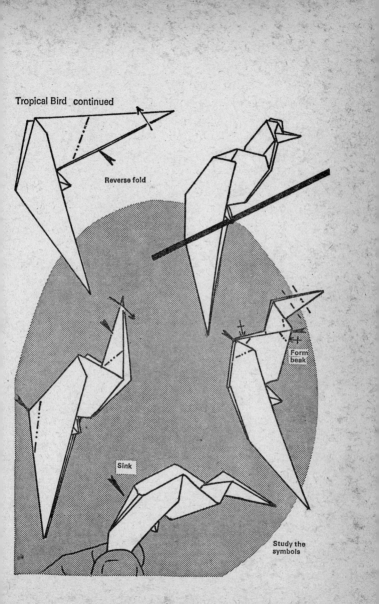

Reverse fold

Form beak

Sink

Study the symbols

67

Xmas Tree . Ligia Montoya   Argentina

Use a square
Fold two sides to middle
and cut along creases

Make two Rabbit's ears
or Fish Base (page 72)

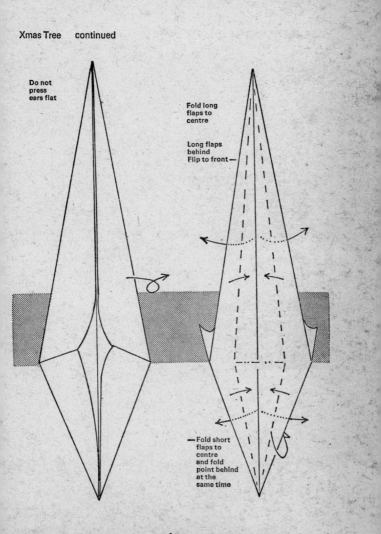

Do not
press
ears flat

Fold long
flaps to
centre

Long flaps
behind
Flip to front —

— Fold short
flaps to
centre
and fold
point behind
at the
same time

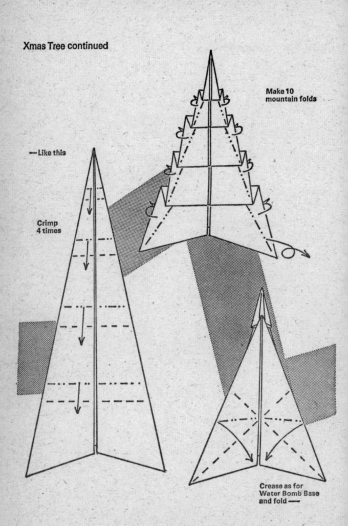

Make 10
mountain folds

— Like this

Crimp
4 times

Crease as for
Water Bomb Base
and fold —

70

Xmas Tree   An immaculate fold

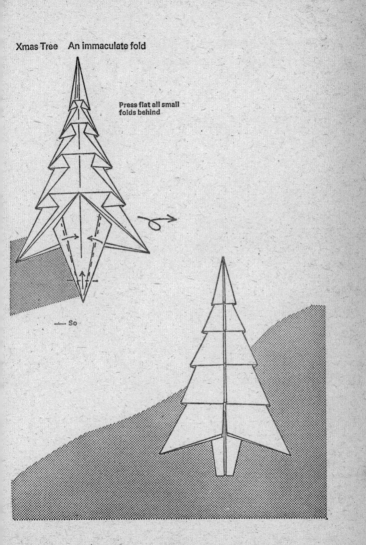

Press flat all small
folds behind

— So

Angel Fish Robert Harbin. England

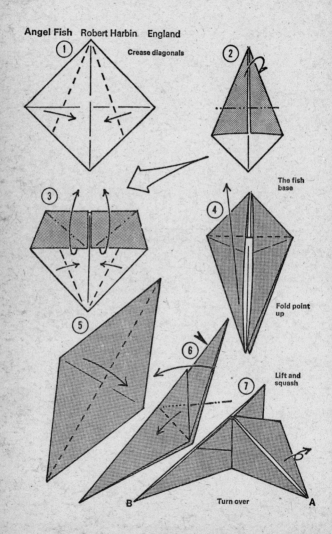

① Crease diagonals

②

The fish base

③

④ Fold point up

⑤

⑥

⑦ Lift and squash

B   Turn over   A

72

Angel Fish continued

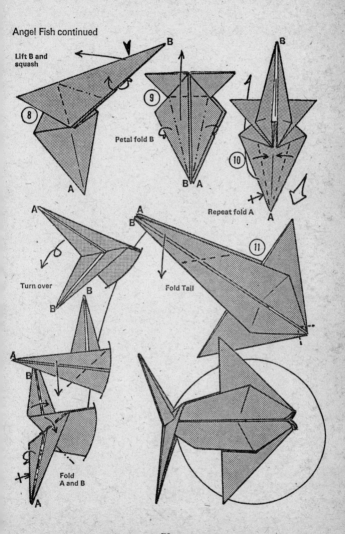

Lift B and squash

⑧

B

A

Petal fold B

⑨

B A

⑩

B

Repeat fold A

A

Turn over

A'

B

B

Fold Tail

A
B

⑪

A
B

Fold A and B

A

Frisbee   Ed Sullivan   U.S.A.

You need 9
8 cm squares
of different
colours

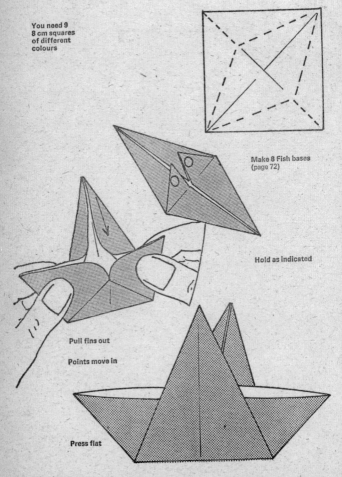

Make 8 Fish bases
(page 72)

Hold as indicated

Pull fins out

Points move in

Press flat

74

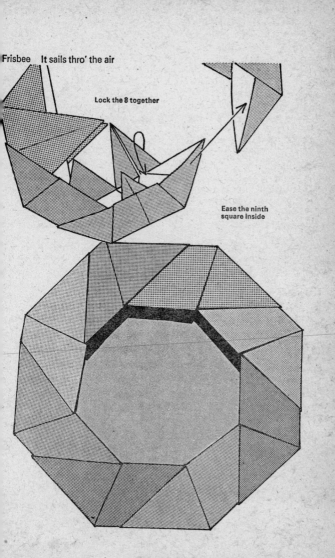

Frisbee   It sails thro' the air

Lock the 8 together

Ease the ninth
square inside

75

Dachshund   Paul Castles   England.

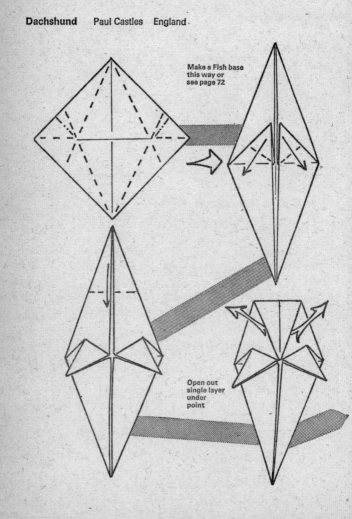

Make a Fish base
this way or
see page 72

Open out
single layer
under
point

Dachshund continued

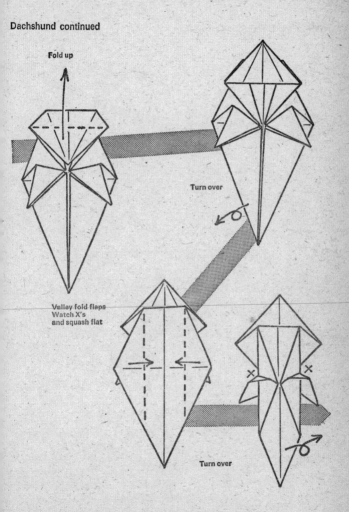

Fold up

Turn over

Valley fold flaps
Watch X's
and squash flat

Turn over

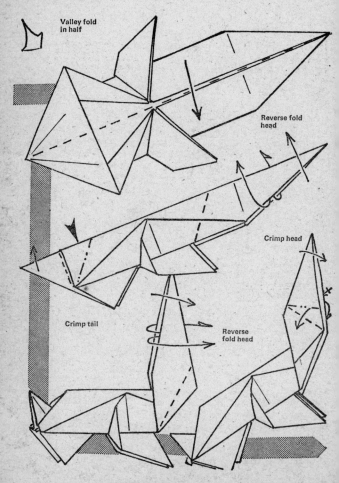

Valley fold
in half

Reverse fold
head

Crimp head

Crimp tail

Reverse
fold head

78

Dachshund continued

Hold as indicated
pull to sink head

79

Neolithic Man   Edward Megrath   England

Crease diagonals
Valley fold flap to
point indicated

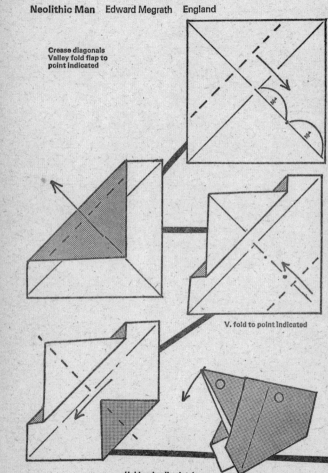

V. fold to point indicated

Hold and pull point down

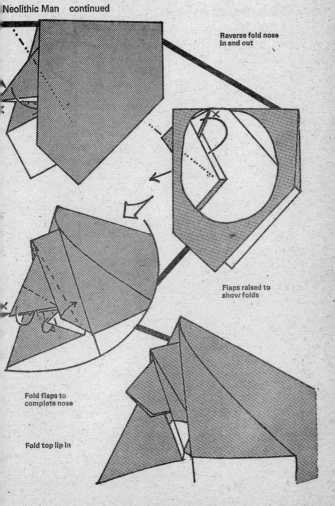

Reverse fold nose
in and out

Flaps raised to
show folds

Fold flaps to
complete nose

Fold top lip in

Neolithic Man　Make the mouth work

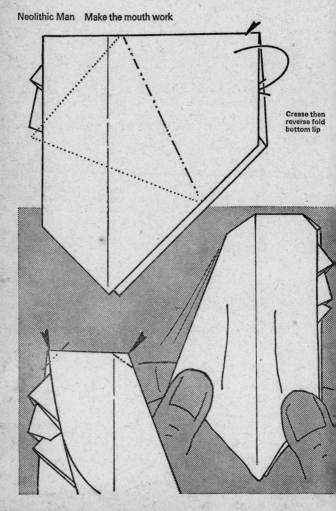

Crease then
reverse fold
bottom lip

82

Seated Cat   Pat Crawford   U.S.A.

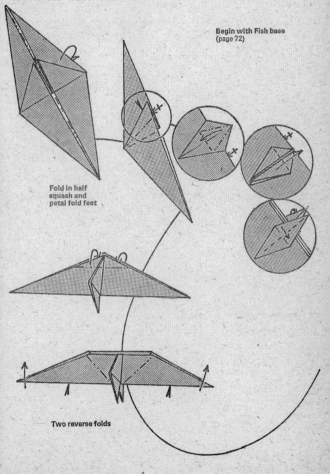

Begin with Fish base
(page 72)

Fold in half
squash and
petal fold feet

Two reverse folds

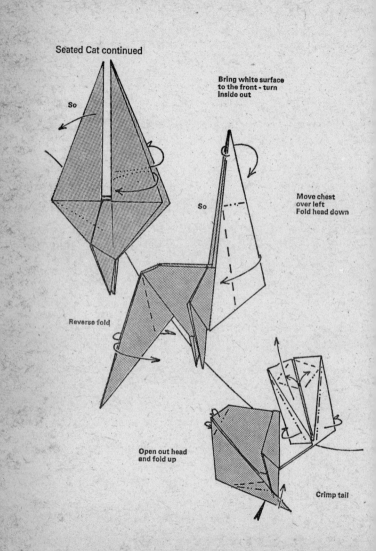

Seated Cat continued

So

Bring white surface
to the front - turn
inside out

So

Move chest
over left
Fold head down

Reverse fold

Open out head
and fold up

Crimp tail

84

Seated Cat continued

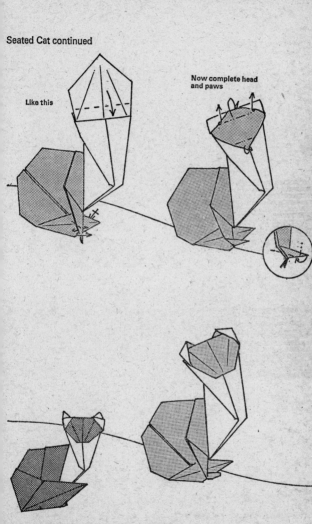

Like this

Now complete head
and paws

Bird Base   A Basic fold

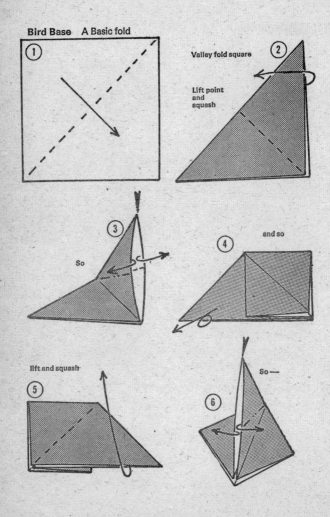

① Valley fold square

② Lift point and squash

③ So

④ and so

⑤ lift and squash

⑥ So —

86

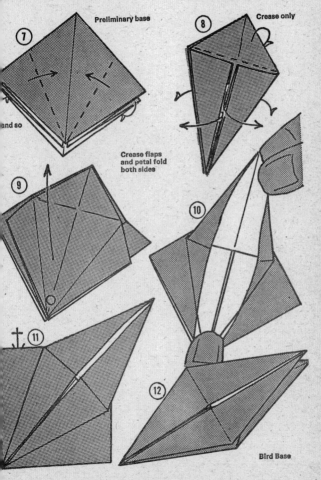

Preliminary base

Crease only

⑦

and so

⑧

Crease flaps
and petal fold
both sides

⑨

⑩

⑪

⑫

Bird Base

Crane Traditional Japanese

Begin with a Bird base (page 86)

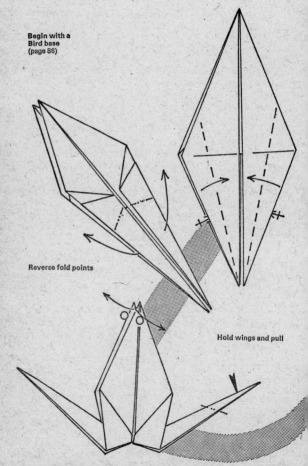

Reverse fold points

Hold wings and pull

88

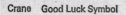
Crane   Good Luck Symbol

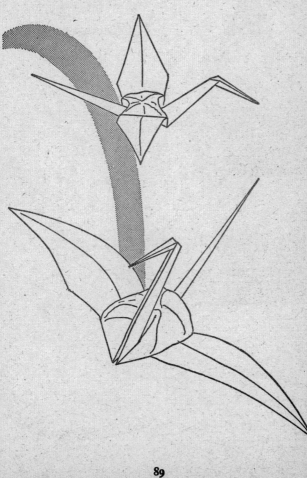

Stretched Bird Base

Begin with the
Bird Base (page 86)

This way up

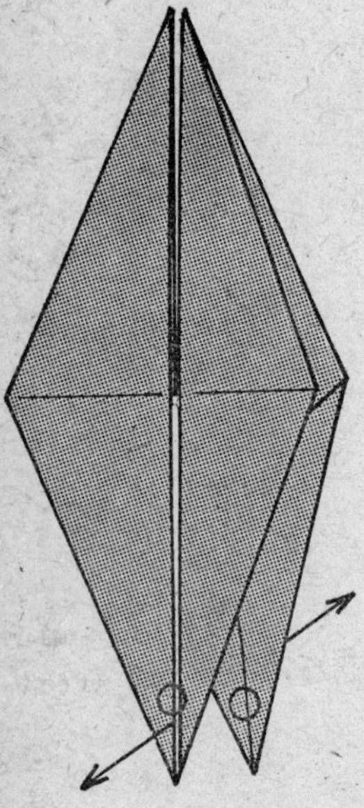

Hold points and stretch

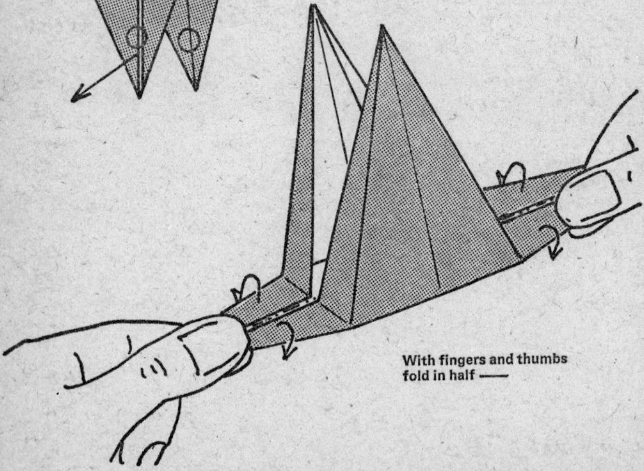

With fingers and thumbs
fold in half ——

Stretched Bird Base continued

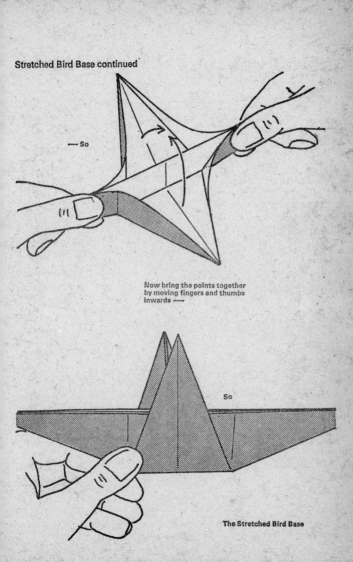

— So

Now bring the points together by moving fingers and thumbs inwards —

So

The Stretched Bird Base

White Walrus   Robert Harbin   England

Start with a
Stretched Bird Base
page 90

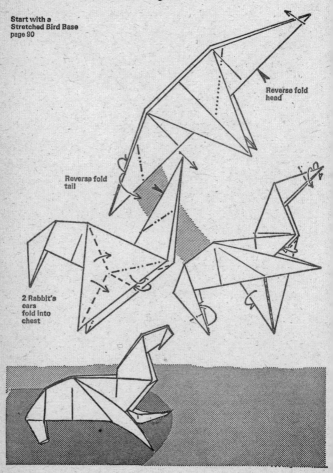

Reverse fold
head

Reverse fold
tail

2 Rabbit's
ears
fold into
chest

Wedding Bells   Mick Guy   England

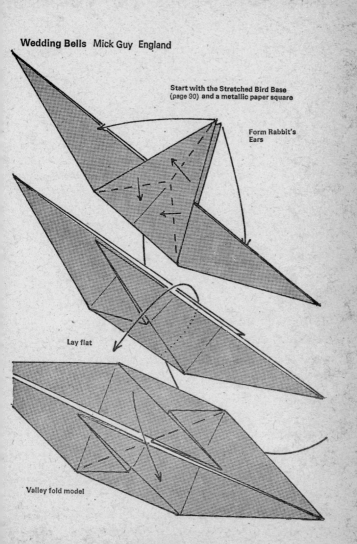

Start with the Stretched Bird Base
(page 90) and a metallic paper square

Form Rabbit's
Ears

Lay flat

Valley fold model

Wedding Bells continued

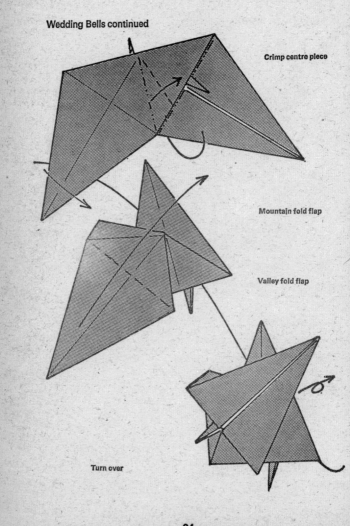

Crimp centre piece

Mountain fold flap

Valley fold flap

Turn over

94

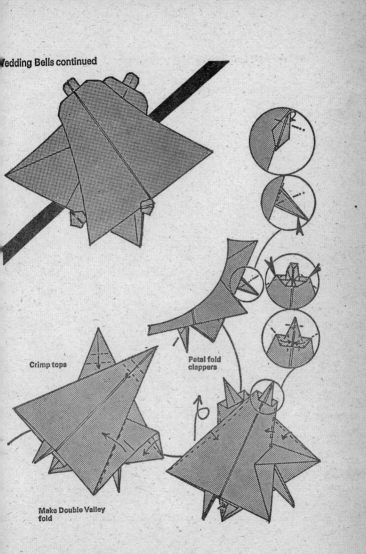

Crimp tops

Petal fold clappers

Make Double Valley fold

95

Boy on a Dolphin   Robert Harbin   England

Begin with Stretched Bird Base
(page 90)

Reverse fold points

Make colour-
change by
turning inside out

So—

96

Boy on a Dolphin continued

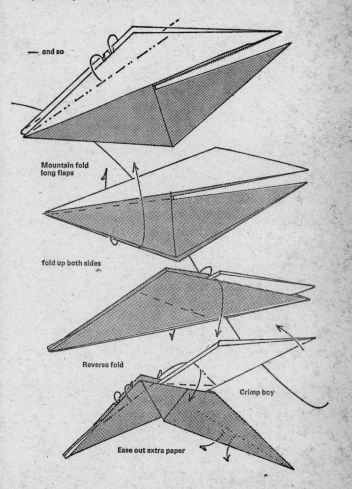

— and so

Mountain fold
long flaps

fold up both sides

Reverse fold

Crimp boy

Ease out extra paper

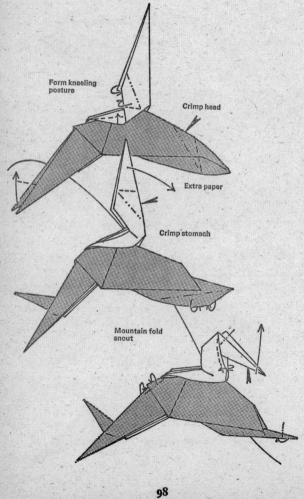

Form kneeling
posture

Crimp head

Extra paper

Crimp stomach

Mountain fold
snout

Complete head

Make Dolphin smile

Robin   Joan Homewood   England

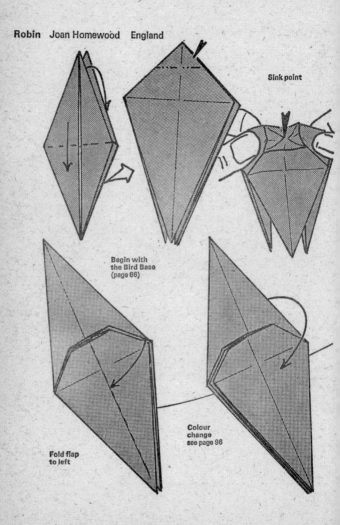

Sink point

Begin with
the Bird Base
(page 86)

Fold flap
to left

Colour
change
see page 96

100

Robin continued

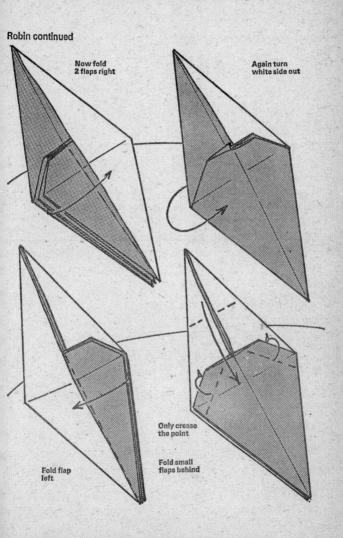

Now fold
2 flaps right

Again turn
white side out

Fold flap
left

Only crease
the point

Fold small
flaps behind

Robin continued

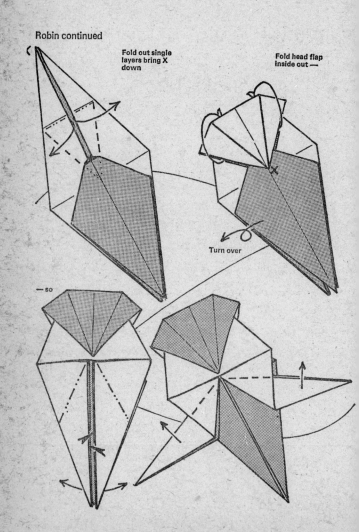

Fold out single
layers bring X
down

Fold head flap
inside out —

Turn over

— so

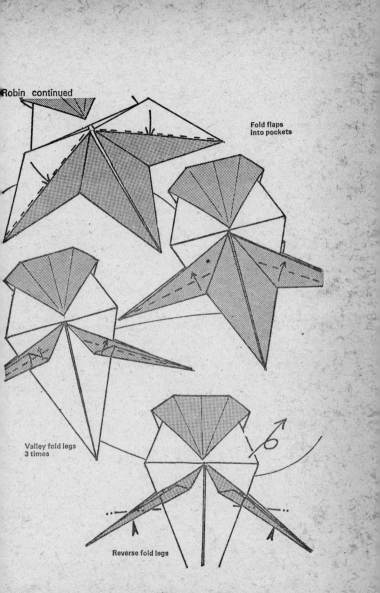

Robin continued

Fold flaps
into pockets

Valley fold legs
3 times

Reverse fold legs

103

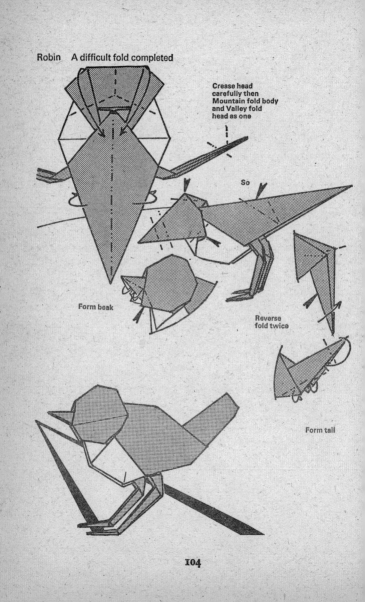

Robin   A difficult fold completed

Crease head
carefully then
Mountain fold body
and Valley fold
head as one

So

Form beak

Reverse
fold twice

Form tail

Super Star

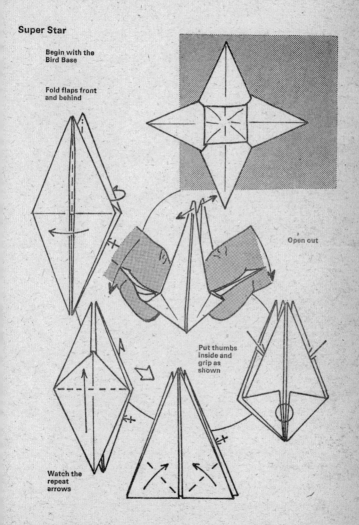

Begin with the Bird Base

Fold flaps front and behind

Open out

Put thumbs inside and grip as shown

Watch the repeat arrows

Dagger Colin Rowe (age 14) England

Begin with Bird Base
(page 100)

Make a
Rabbit's Ear

and again

So

Fold flaps flat

Fold 4 flaps

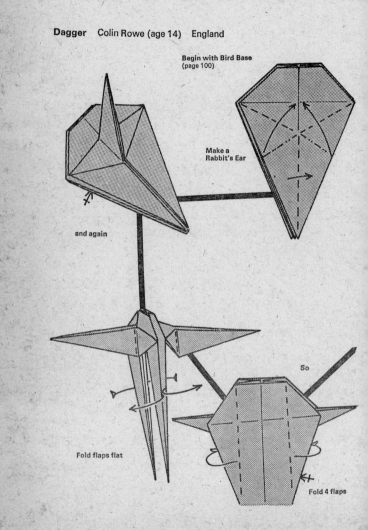

Dagger   A fine bookmarker this

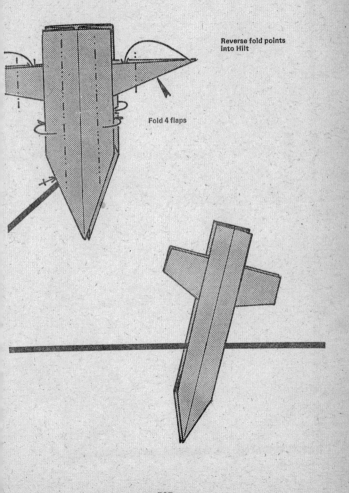

Reverse fold points
into Hilt

Fold 4 flaps

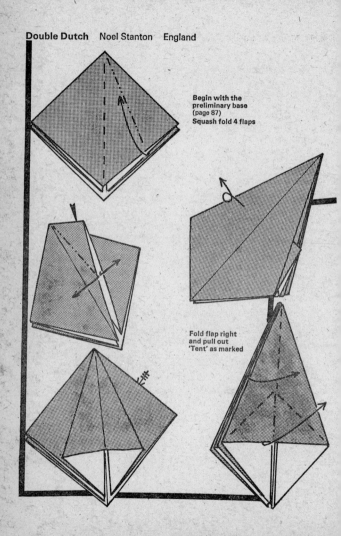

Double Dutch Noel Stanton England

Begin with the
preliminary base
(page 87)
Squash fold 4 flaps

Fold flap right
and pull out
'Tent' as marked

108

Double Dutch continued

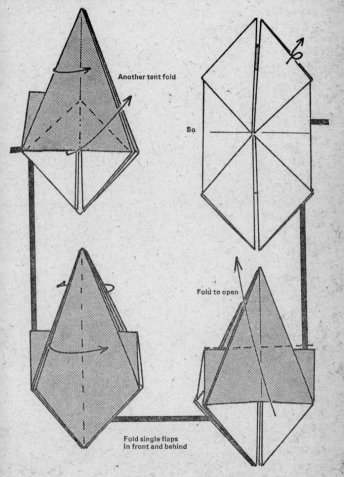

Another tent fold

So

Fold to open

Fold single flaps
in front and behind

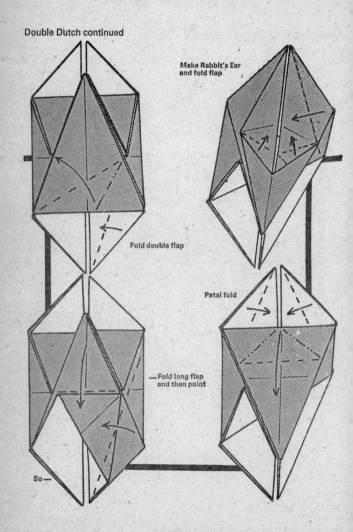

Double Dutch continued

Make Rabbit's Ear
and fold flap

Fold double flap

Petal fold

Fold long flap
and then point

So —

110

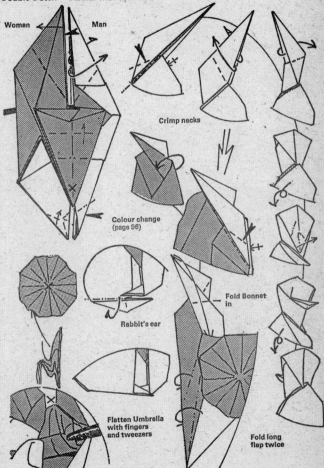

Double Dutch Careful with the heads

Woman Man

Crimp necks

Colour change
(page 96)

Rabbit's ear

Fold Bonnet in

Flatten Umbrella
with fingers
and tweezers

Fold long
flap twice

Double Dutch   Very difficult   Try again

Clerical Hat   Ligia Montoya   Argentina

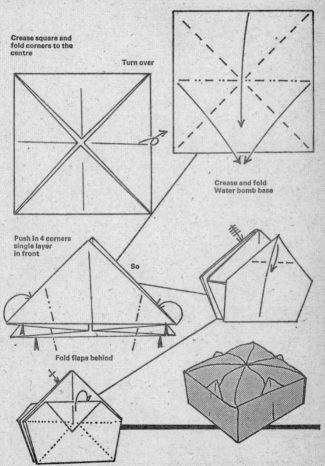

Crease square and fold corners to the centre

Turn over

Crease and fold Water bomb base

Push in 4 corners single layer in front

So

Fold flaps behind

113

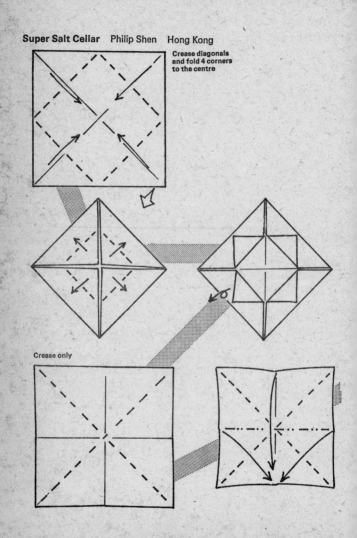

Crease diagonals
and fold 4 corners
to the centre

Crease only

114

Super Salt Cellar continued

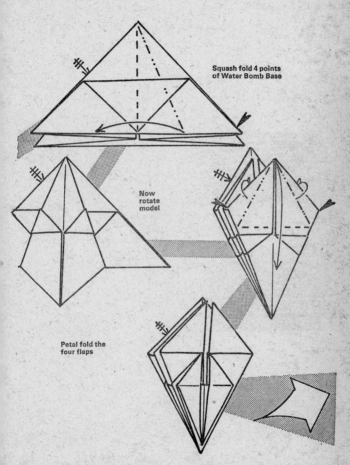

Squash fold 4 points
of Water Bomb Base

Now
rotate
model

Petal fold the
four flaps

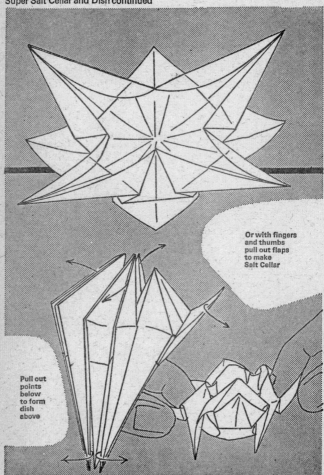

Or with fingers
and thumbs
pull out flaps
to make
Salt Cellar

Pull out
points
below
to form
dish
above

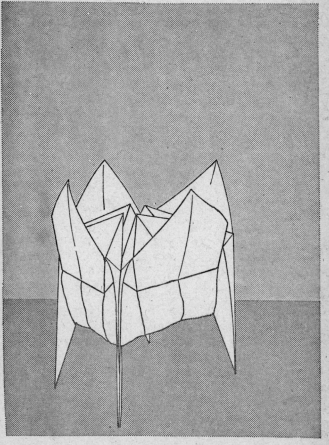

Moth   Tim Ward   England

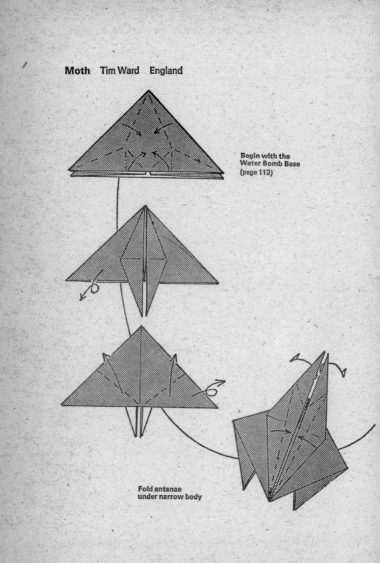

Begin with the
Water Bomb Base
(page 113)

Fold antenae
under narrow body

Moth continued

Shapes and the Windmill Base

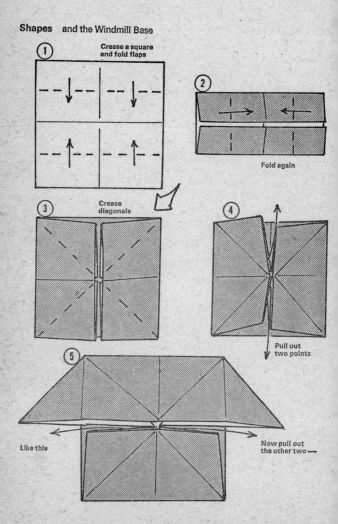

① Crease a square and fold flaps

② Fold again

③ Crease diagonals

④ Pull out two points

⑤ Like this

Now pull out the other two —

The Windmill Base continued

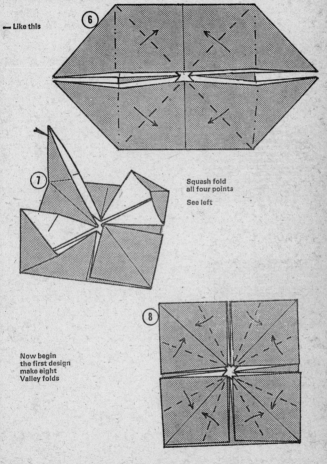

⑥

⑦

Squash fold
all four points

See left

⑧

Now begin
the first design
make eight
Valley folds

Shapes   This is Doodling

Squash fold 8 corners

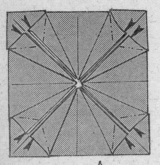

Mountain and Valley fold corners and points

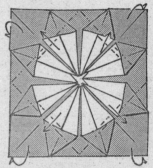

Stop here if you wish

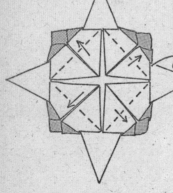

You could stop here but go ahead and fold corners

Fold 4 corners to make feet

Shapes   Most of them make boxes

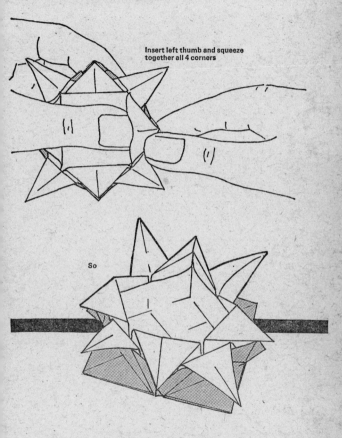

Insert left thumb and squeeze
together all 4 corners

So

Persian Helmet   Ligia Montoya   Argentina

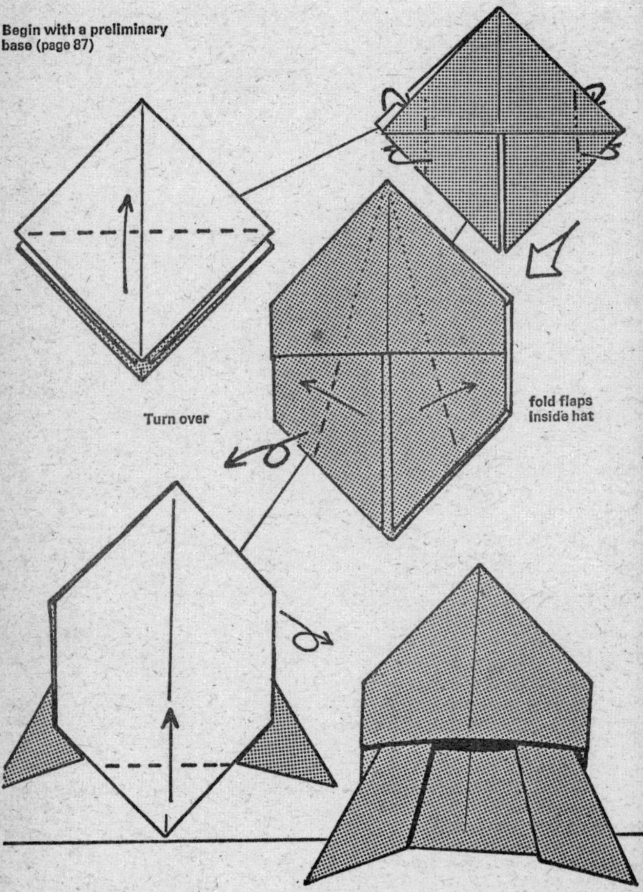

Begin with a preliminary
base (page 87)

Turn over

fold flaps
inside hat

Jackstone   Jack Skillman   U.S.A.

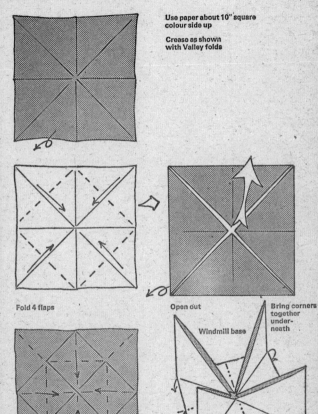

Use paper about 10" square
colour side up

Crease as shown
with Valley folds

Fold 4 flaps

Open out

Windmill base

Bring corners
together
under-
neath

Fold sides to middle

125

Jackstone First published in the Origamian

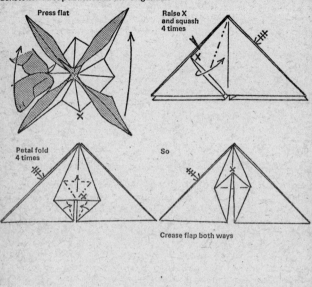

Press flat

**Raise X
and squash
4 times**

**Petal fold
4 times**

So

Crease flap both ways

and so

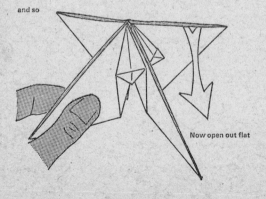

Now open out flat

126

Jackstone Pre-creasing

When opened out leave in creases

Now carefully Mountain and Valley fold
as indicated

Corner by corner press together (Mountain fold)
at the points shown

Careful manipulation will make model
take shape

Here you see two corners in action
and the diamond shapes forming

Move to the other two corners
and persevere—

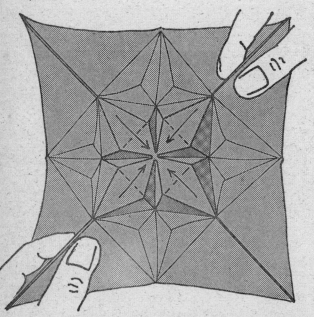

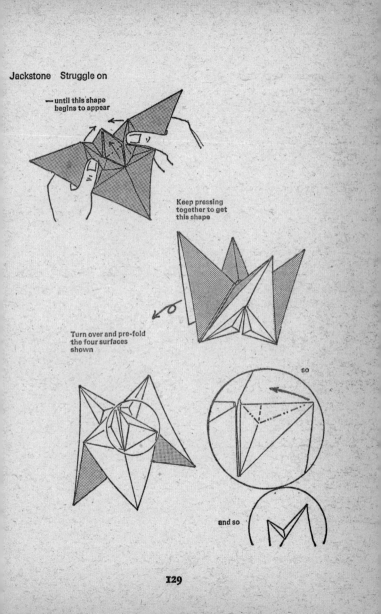

Jackstone   Struggle on

— until this shape
begins to appear

Keep pressing
together to get
this shape

Turn over and pre-fold
the four surfaces
shown

so

and so

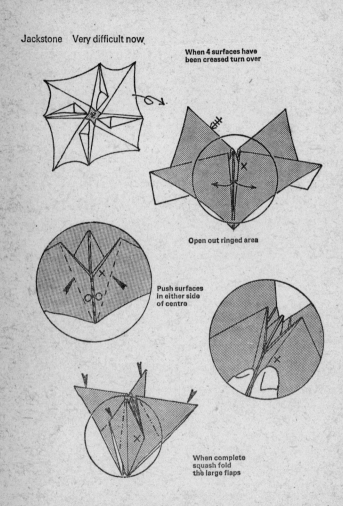

Jackstone   Very difficult now

When 4 surfaces have
been creased turn over

Open out ringed area

Push surfaces
in either side
of centre

When complete
squash fold
the large flaps

130

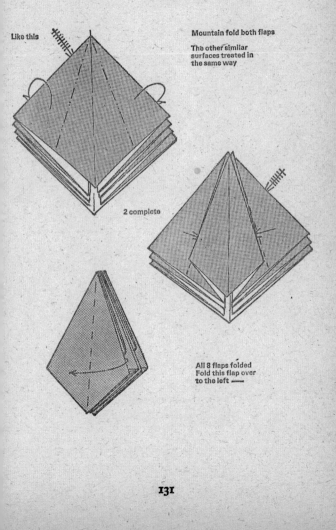

Like this

Mountain fold both flaps

The other similar
surfaces treated in
the same way

2 complete

All 8 flaps folded
Fold this flap over
to the left ⟶

Put 8 flaps into 4 pockets

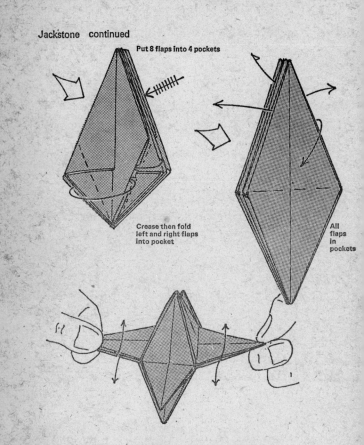

Crease then fold
left and right flaps
into pocket

All
flaps
in
pockets

Now ease and pull out the 4 points
Middle becomes 3D
Now hold the middle and 3D the other
4 points ──

Jackstone   You deserve a medal

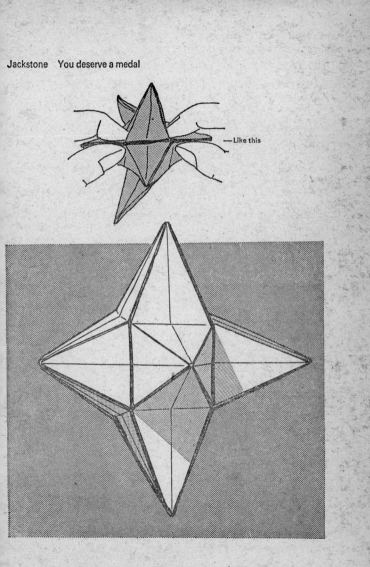

—Like this

Basket Japanese Donated by Lillian Oppenheimer

Cut ¼ off a square

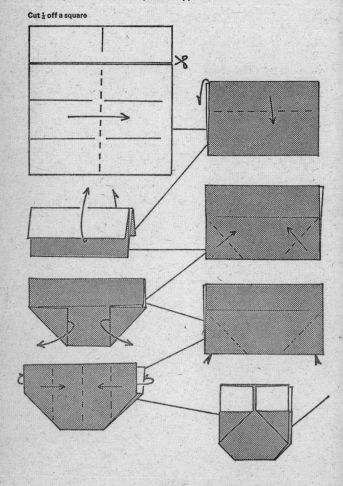

Basket continued

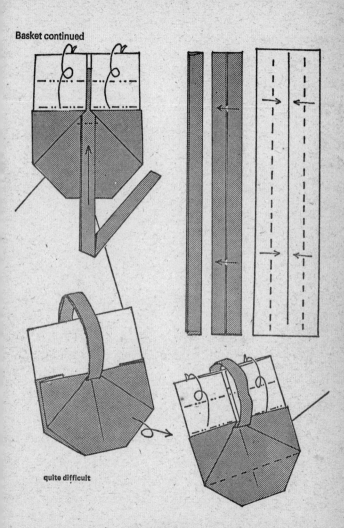

quite difficult

136

Knight in Armour   Neal Elias   U.S.A.

Large silver
foil square

Crease and
fold flaps

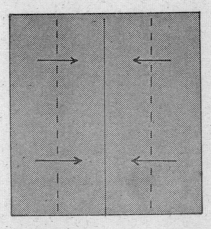

Complete folds and crease corners

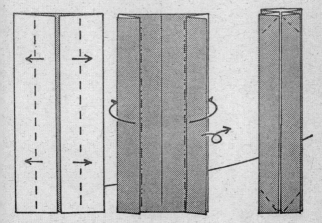

Elias' special base for figures

Sink the creased corners

So

The Base completed grip the points below——

Top view

Hold and pull all 4 corners to the middle by stretching

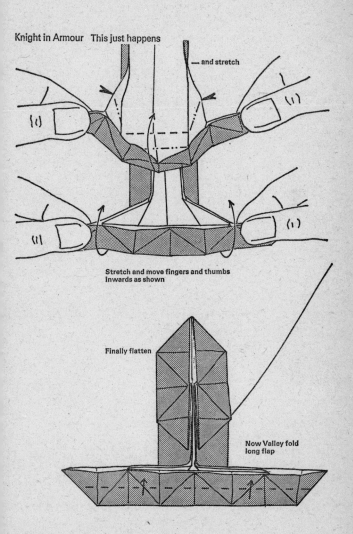

Knight in Armour This just happens

— and stretch

{(

(}

{(

(}

(}

(}

Stretch and move fingers and thumbs
inwards as shown

Finally flatten

Now Valley fold
long flap

Knight in Armour   Don't be afraid of this

Hold legs and fold inwards
open body and fold skirt
behind legs

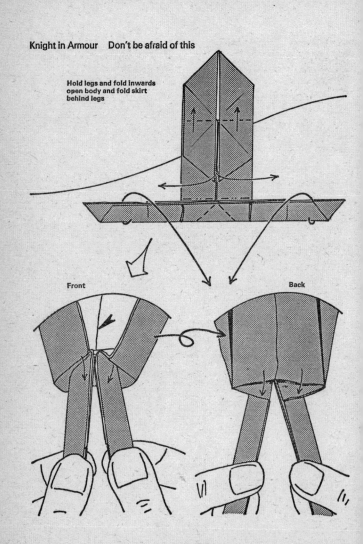

Front

Back

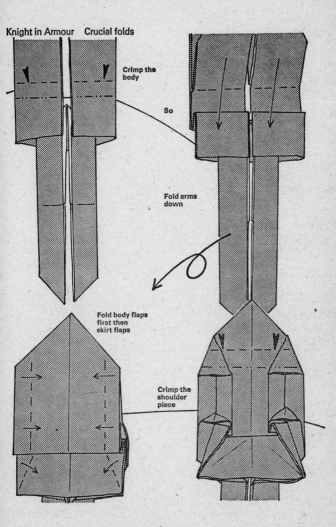

Knight in Armour   Crucial folds

Crimp the
body

So

Fold arms
down

Fold body flaps
first then
skirt flaps

Crimp the
shoulder
piece

Knight in Armour   Special care

Make special crimps to form arms

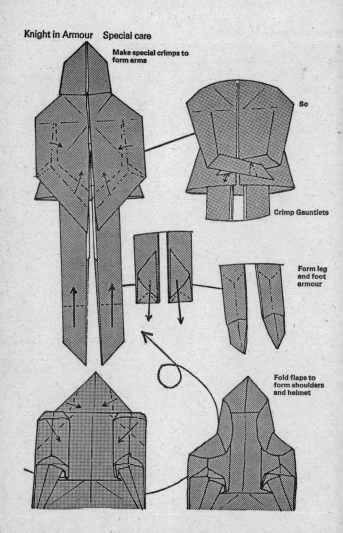

Sc

Crimp Gauntlets

Form leg and foot armour

Fold flaps to form shoulders and helmet

Skier   Robert Harbin   England

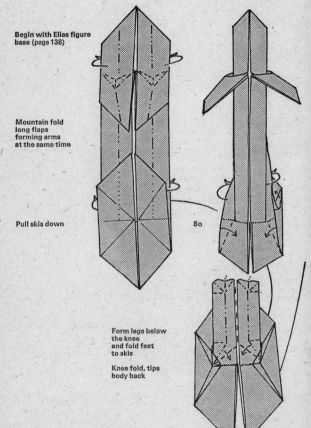

Begin with Elias figure
base (page 138)

Mountain fold
long flaps
forming arms
at the same time

Pull skis down

So

Form legs below
the knee
and fold feet
to skis

Knee fold, tips
body back

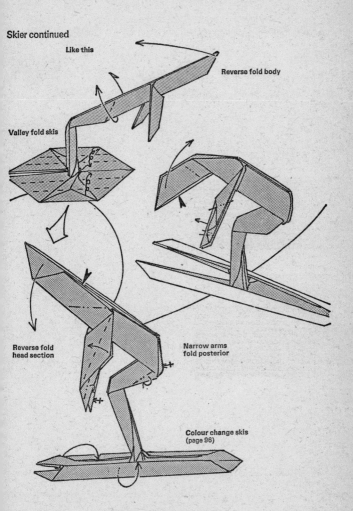

Like this

Reverse fold body

Valley fold skis

Reverse fold
head section

Narrow arms
fold posterior

Colour change skis
(page 96)

145

Form the woollen cap

Make small fold for face

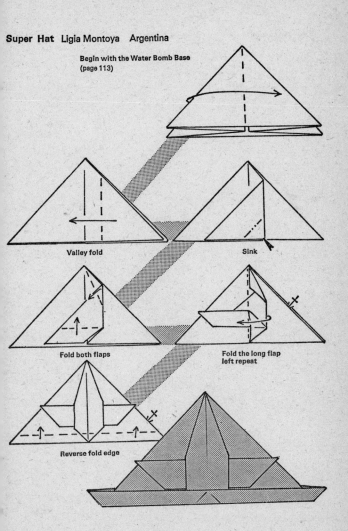

Super Hat Ligia Montoya   Argentina

Begin with the Water Bomb Base
(page 113)

Valley fold

Sink

Fold both flaps

Fold the long flap
left repeat

Reverse fold edge

Flower and Leaf Toshie Takahama Tokyo

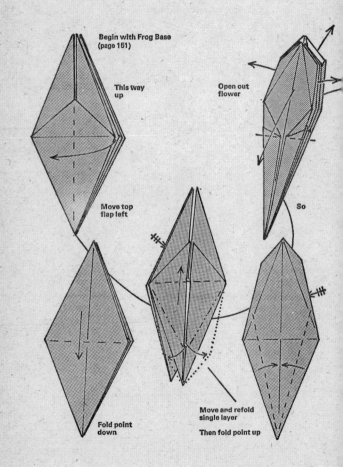

Begin with Frog Base
(page 151)

This way
up

Open out
flower

Move top
flap left

So

Fold point
down

Move and refold
single layer

Then fold point up

So

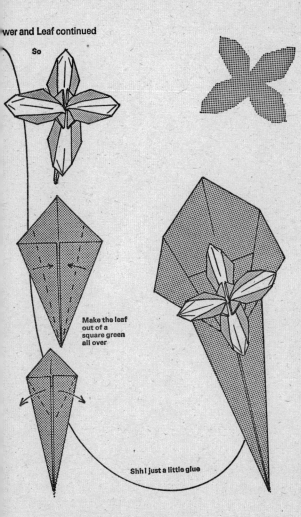

Make the leaf
out of a
square green
all over

Shh! just a little glue

149

Plumed Helmet   Ligia Montoya   Argentina

Begin with the Water Bomb Base
(page 113)

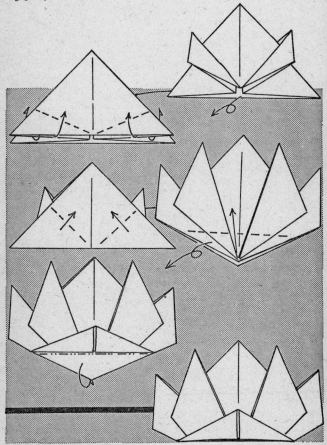

Old Kentucky Horse   Raymond K. M'Lain   U.S.A.

Begin with the preliminary base
(page 87)

Squash fold 4 corners

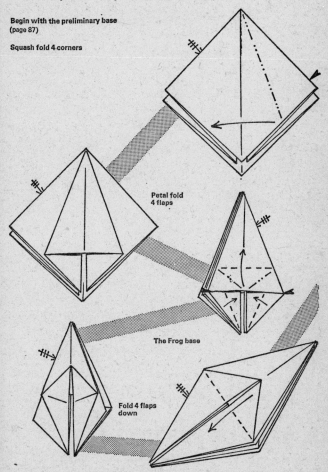

Petal fold
4 flaps

The Frog base

Fold 4 flaps
down

So

Tuck triangle
inside front
and back

Hold points
indicated and
pull to do this

So

Now open out
completely and
turn upside down

Pinch
together
at points
indicated
and push
together —

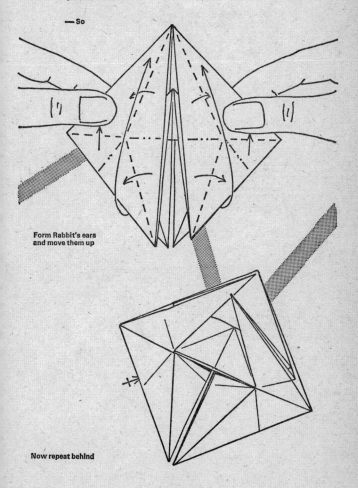

Old Kentucky Horse continued

— So

Form Rabbit's ears
and move them up

Now repeat behind

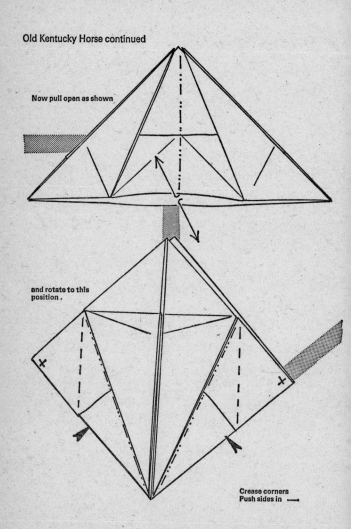

Now pull open as shown

and rotate to this
position .

Crease corners
Push sides in ━━

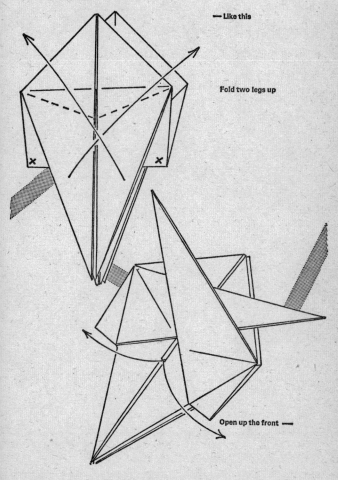

— Like this

Fold two legs up

Open up the front —

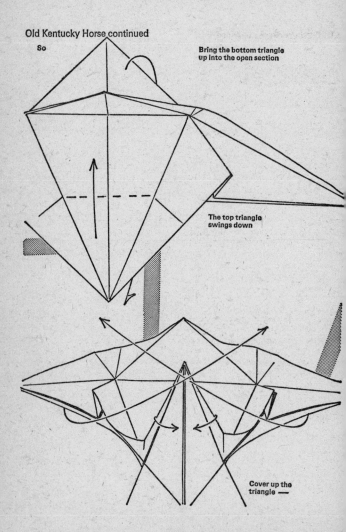

So

Bring the bottom triangle
up into the open section

The top triangle
swings down

Cover up the
triangle —

Old Kentucky Horse continued

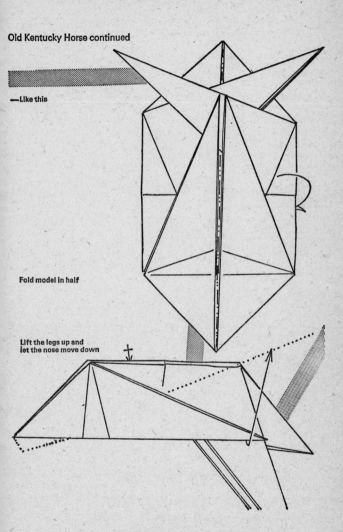

—Like this

Fold model in half

Lift the legs up and
let the nose move down

Old Kentucky Horse continued

Nose down

Tuck X on both sides into
the pocket behind

Legs folded down and
X tucked behind

Now squash fold legs ──

158

Old Kentucky Horse continued

— Like this

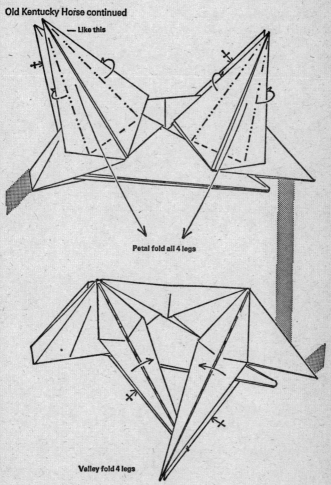

Petal fold all 4 legs

Valley fold 4 legs

Old Kentucky Horse continued

Fold head flap under when eased from behind leg

Below turn inside out
(colour change page 96)

Both hind legs X

This flap also - then fold leg right

Like this

Reverse fold both points

Fold flaps into body

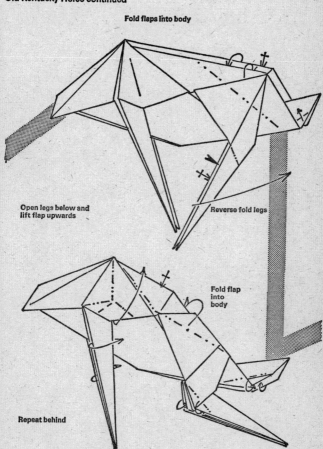

**Open legs below and
lift flap upwards**

Reverse fold legs

**Fold flap
into
body**

Repeat behind

Old Kentucky Horse continued

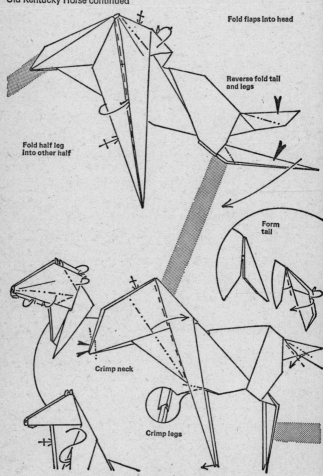

Fold flaps into head

Reverse fold tail
and legs

Fold half leg
into other half

Form
tail

Crimp neck

Crimp legs

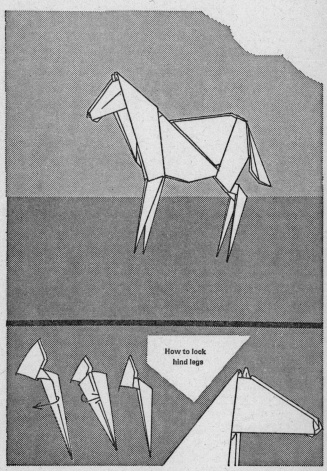

How to lock
hind legs

Kangaroo E. G. Langridle England

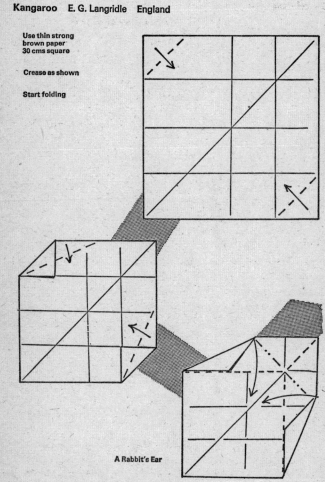

Use thin strong
brown paper
30 cms square

Crease as shown

Start folding

A Rabbit's Ear

Kangaroo continued

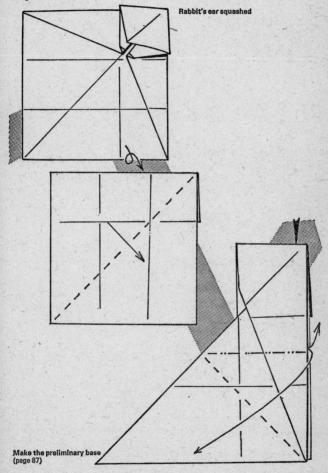

Rabbit's ear squashed

Make the preliminary base
(page 87)

Kangaroo continued

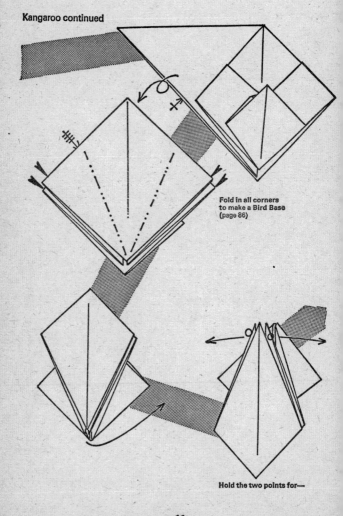

Fold in all corners
to make a Bird Base
(page 86)

Hold the two points for—

166

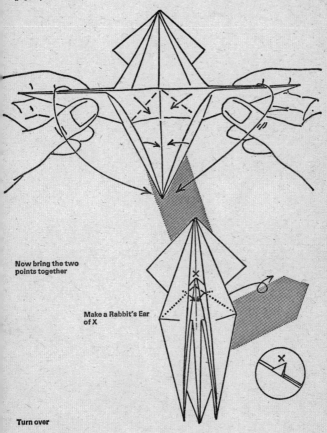

a Stretched Bird Base
(page 90)

Now bring the two
points together

Make a Rabbit's Ear
of X

Turn over

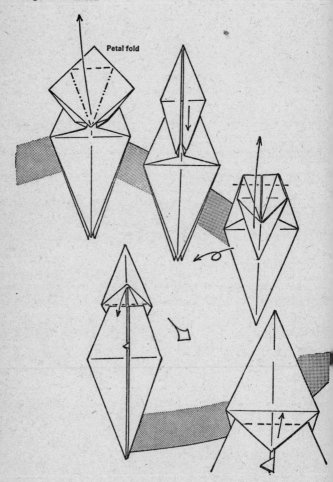

Petal fold

Kangaroo continued

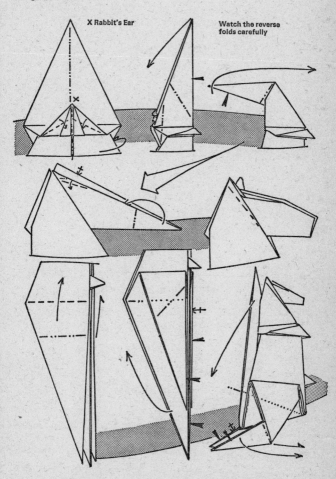

X Rabbit's Ear

Watch the reverse
folds carefully

Finishing touches
Look for every symbol

Kangaroo   traced from the original

Medieval Hat Robert Harbin England

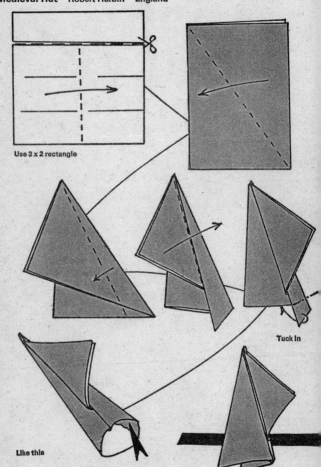

Use 3 x 2 rectangle

Tuck in

Like this

With this unique base
Fred Rhom has produced
many masterpieces

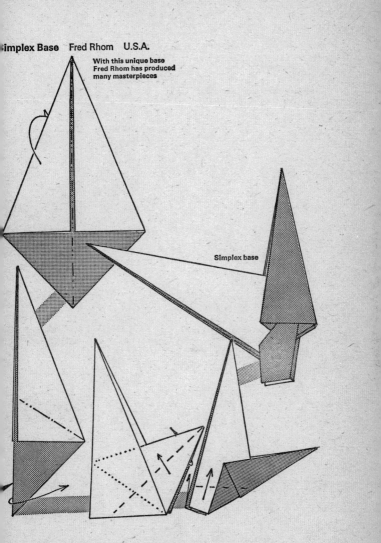

Simplex base

173

Snake Charmer Fred Rohm U.S.A.

Begin with the Simplex Base
(page 173)

Begin with colour side up
Use metallic foil

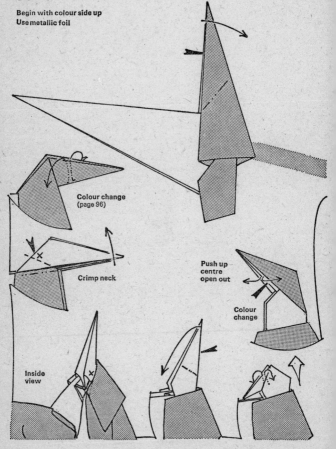

Colour change
(page 96)

Crimp neck

Push up
centre
open out

Colour
change

Inside
view

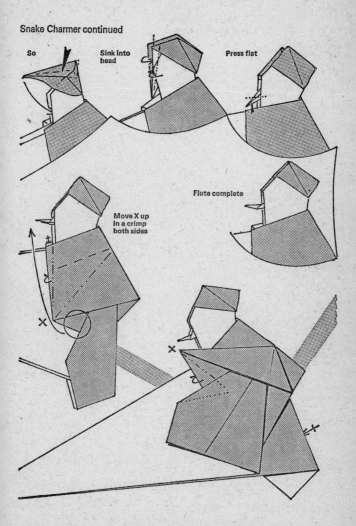

So

Sink into head

Press flat

Flute complete

Move X up in a crimp both sides

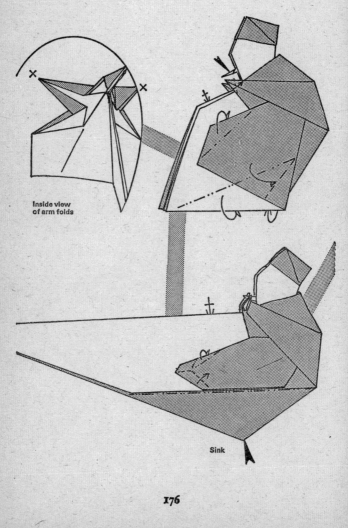

Inside view
of arm folds

Sink

Snake Charmer continued

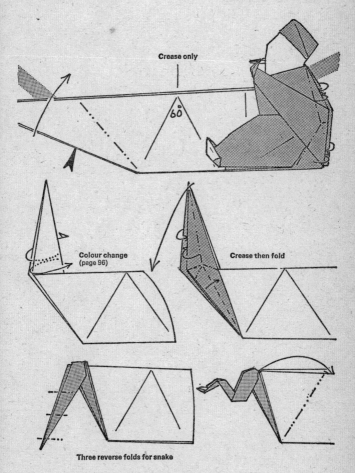

Crease only

60°

Colour change
(page 96)

Crease then fold

Three reverse folds for snake

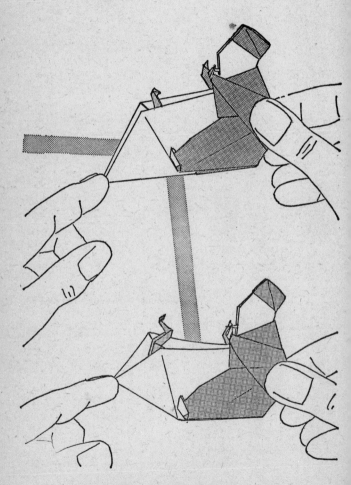

Hat and Fox Puppet   Japanese

Crease a square and fold in half
Squash fold flaps

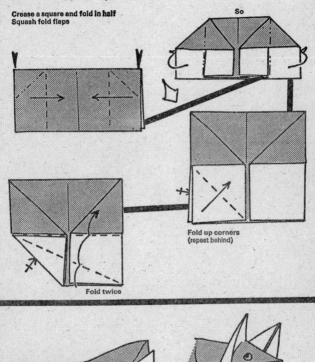

So

Fold up corners
(repeat behind)

Fold twice

Otomo Nu Koronushi   From the Kan No Mado

A white square traditionally
precoloured
Cut as shown
Make poet and colour
afterwards

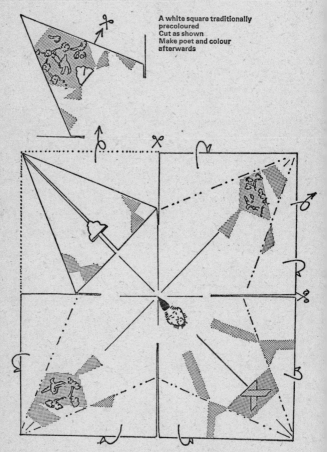

Otomo Nu Koronushi Folded from ancient drawings by Sydney French   England

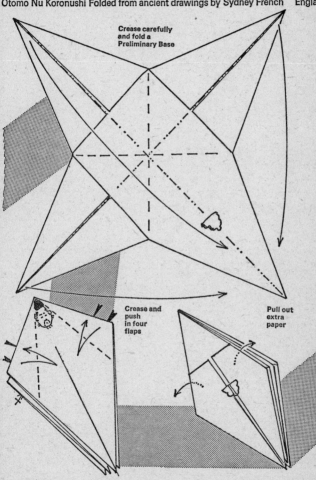

Crease carefully
and fold a
Preliminary Base

Crease and
push
in four
flaps

Pull out
extra
paper

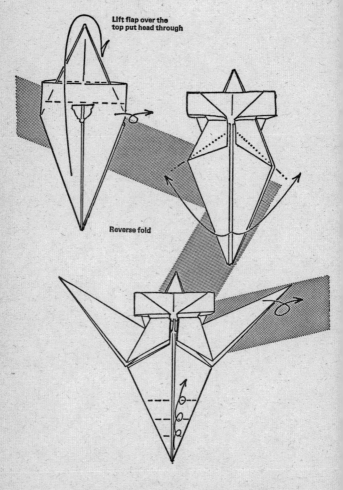

Lift flap over the
top put head through

Reverse fold

Otomo No Koronushi continued

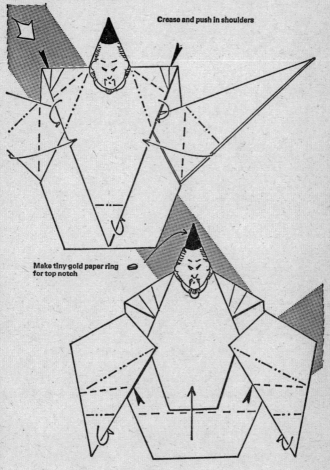

Crease and push in shoulders

Make tiny gold paper ring for top notch

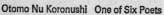 Otomo Nu Koronushi One of Six Poets

The End

BIBLIOGRAPHY

Here are the titles of books on Origami which are fairly easy to obtain.

HARBIN, Robert. *Secrets of Origami*, Oldbourne Press, London (1963).
One hundred and fifty models, 1,400 drawings, and 70 photographs. The world's leading folders have contributed original models to this anthology, which also contains a large selection of traditional folds. This book obtainable from libraries is at the moment being republished.

— *Paper Magic*, Oldbourne Press, London (1956).
This book contains more than one hundred folds and is ideal for the beginner and collector. Republished by John Maxfield Ltd., London.

— *Origami*, Hodder Paperbacks (1969).
A comprehensive collection of paper-folds from all over the world. Hundreds of drawings which lead you step by step through simple and complicated models. A bestseller available almost anywhere.

KENNEWAY, Eric. *Simple Origami*, Dryad Press, Leicester (1970).
A neat, clearly illustrated paperback with many photographs of original models. Available everywhere.

RANDLETT, Samuel. *The Art of Origami*, E. P. Dutton Inc., New York. British Edition, Faber and Faber, London (1961).
A really fine book for both beginner and expert. Traditional and original folds are superbly illustrated by Jean Randlett. Obtainable in England and America.

— *The Best of Origami; New Models by Contemporary Folders*, E. P. Dutton, Inc., New York. British Edition, Faber and Faber, London (1963).
This book is an absolute 'must'. The models are quite outstanding, and the material in this book cannot be found elsewhere. Perfect in every way. Obtainable in America only.

LEWIS, Shari, and OPPENHEIMER, Lillian. *Folding Paper Puppets; Folding Paper Toys*, Stein and Day, New York. Puppets (1962), Toys (1963).
Here are two beautifully illustrated books (obtainable

almost everywhere) of simple models that work. Splendid for entertaining the young.

YOSHIZAWA, Akira. Books by this author are printed in Japan and can be obtained from The Origami Centre in New York. Printed in Japanese language, but with detailed illustrations easily understood by the initiated. Obtainable from the Origami Centre, New York.

HONDA, Isao, Editor, Japan Publications Trading Company Ltd., Central P.O., Box 722, Tokyo, Japan.
Mr. Honda has a great number of books to his credit. They are written in English, and are obtainable almost everywhere.

TAKAHAMA, Toshie. *Creative Life with Creative Origami*, Mako-sha Publishing Co., Ltd., Tokyo.
A beautifully illustrated book on Japanese Origami with many original folds, a book you will want to own. British Origami Society or Origami Centre, New York, could get this for you.

UCHIYAMA, Okimasa. *Origami Zukan* (Picture Book of Origami), Hikari no Kuni, Tokyo, Japan (1958).
A really fine work on cut and uncut Origami, considered the best book of its kind in Japan. It is not necessary to understand Japanese, as the diagrams and symbols are the standard ones and are sufficiently clear. Obtainable from the Origami Centre, New York.

SOONG, Maying. *Chinese Paper Folding*, Thames and Hudson, London (1955).
A collection of very clearly illustrated traditional folds, ideal for the beginner and collector. Easily obtainable.

MONTERO, N. *El Mundo de Papel*, Valladolid: Editorian Sever-Cuesta (1939).
Available from the author, at Plaza Campillo 3, Valladolid, Spain, price thirty-eight new pence, or one dollar.

SALVATELLA, Miguel (editor). *Un Hoja de Papel*.
A fine collection of 80 models in illustrations only. Obtainable from the author, at Santo Domingo 5, Barcelona, Spain, price thirty-eight new pence, or one dollar.

Most booksellers and big stores seem to stock a few Origami books, and it is a good idea to build up a small library by seeing what one can find in the shops.